COMFORT

COMFORT
A PHILOSOPHICAL DIALOGUE

Nicholas J. Pappas

Algora Publishing
New York

Names: Pappas, Nicholas J., author.
Title: Comfort : a philosophical dialogue / Nicholas J. Pappas.
Description: New York : Algora Publishing, [2023] | Summary: "Two acquaintances
are awaiting the results of surgery on friends. Through a wide-ranging conversation
touching on fear, laughter, spirit, belief, and other topics, they make clear that we can
do far more than simply wait, passively, in fear of results. With the right person, you can,
together, drink in life—and drink deeply indeed."   Provided by publisher.

Identifiers: Library of Congress Control Number: 2023951455

ISBN 9781628945270 (trade paperback) | ISBN 9781628945287 (hardcover) | ISBN
9781628945294 (pdf)

Printed in the United States

More Books by Nick Pappas
from Algora Publishing

Controvert, or On the Lie and Other Philosophical Dialogues, 2008

Aristocrat, and The Community: Two Philosophical Dialogues, 2010

On Awareness: A Collection of Philosophical Dialogues, 2011

Belief and Integrity: Philosophical Dialogues, 2011

On Strength, 2012

On Freedom: A Philosophical Dialogue, 2014

On Life: Philosophical Dialogues, 2015

On Love: A Philosophical Dialogue, 2016

On Destiny: A Philosophical Dialogue, 2016

On Wisdom: A Philosophical Dialogue, 2017

All of Health: A Philosophical Dialogue, 2018

On Education: A Philosophical Dialogue, 2018

On Power: A Philosophical Dialogue, 2019

On Ideas: A Philosophical Dialogue, 2020

On Passivity: A Philosophical Dialogue, 2021

On Authority: A Philosophical Dialogue, 2021

On Violence: A Philosophical Dialogue, 2022

Looks: A Philosophical Dialogue, 2022

Rule: A Philosophical Dialogue, 2023

Table of Contents

COMFORT

Characters:
 Director
 Woman

Setting:
 Hospital waiting room

AFRAID

Woman: It was a heart attack.

Director: Ah, it's the same with my friend. Immediate surgery, too.

Woman: Are you afraid?

Director: I don't want to lose my friend. Are you afraid?

Woman: I am. It may seem strange to say, but we can take comfort in each
 other's fear.

Director: How so?

Woman: The greatest fear comes when we're alone.

Director: I disagree.

Woman: You disagree? How?

Director: The greatest fear comes when we're alone, sure—but when we're alone among others.

Woman: You're not afraid when you're completely alone?

Director: I'm not.

Woman: Then I need to learn something from you! But don't you find others to be a distraction? Oh, wait. For that you'd have to be afraid when you're alone. It seems I'm not thinking clearly right now.

Director: Is it because you're afraid?

Woman: Yes. But you can't tell me that you think clearly when you're afraid, can you?

Director: Sometimes fear is a great motivator for thought.

Woman: My mind just shuts down. How is it otherwise with you?

Director: Fear is a torch applied to a frozen soul.

Woman: Ha! You really made me laugh!

Director: Why?

Woman: Because the opposite is true! Fear freezes the soul.

Director: But haven't you heard?

Woman: Heard what?

Director: That severe cold burns just like severe heat?

Woman: You can't tell the difference between the two?

Director: That's what they say.

Woman: You don't strike me as someone who cares what they say.

Director: And you don't seem that way to me, either.

Woman: So what do *we* say?

Director: That we prefer to be hot when it's cold, and cold when it's hot.

Woman: Contrarians?

Director: Seekers after comfort.

Woman: But if we're hot or cold what comfort do we have?

Director: The comfort is in the seeking. We throw ourselves into the snow or sun.

Woman: We seek the opposite of how we feel?

Director: If we feel fear, what do we seek?

Woman: I seek comfort. And you?

Director: I seek to destroy the source of the fear.

Woman: You're really making me laugh!

Director: Laughter is better than fear.

Woman: So long as it's not... *nervous* laughter.

LAUGHTER

Director: I despise nervous laughter.

Woman: Oh, but that's really not nice. People can't help themselves at times.

Director: I know. That's why I despise those who make them feel that way.

Woman: Well, hold on. What makes them feel nervous?

Director: Well, what makes anyone nervous?

Woman: Fear. What do these people fear?

Director: Being exposed.

Woman: As what?

Director: Fakes.

Woman: You mean they pretend to be something they're not.

Director: That's how it seems to me now.

Woman: Why do you think people pretend?

Director: I think it's a sort of short-cut.

Woman: To what?

Director: Success.

Woman: I disagree.

Director: Oh? What do *you* think?

Woman: Some people pretend in order to cover up weakness. Will you tell me you despise weakness?

Director: No.

Woman: So you don't despise when such people laugh?

Director: I love when such people laugh—but not nervously.

Woman: There's comfort in true laughter, isn't there.

Director: Yes, there is. And what's wonderful is that it's unexpected.

Woman: It leaves a sort of glow.

Director: It does. But sometimes people take it too far.

Woman: They laugh and laugh again until it becomes fake.

Director: Precisely.

Woman: They want to hold on to that fleeting comfort.

Director: That's what some people do.

Woman: They should respect the laugh and laugh no more.

Director: I couldn't have said it better myself.

Woman: Yes, but you lied.

Director: Did I?

Woman: You said you despise those who make people laugh nervously. You don't despise *all* of them. You despise those who harass the weak.

Director: Are you saying some of the strong are fakes?

Woman: Ha! You know it's true!

Director: You're right. I like to see them squirm.

Woman: So do I. There's something comforting in that.

Director: Justice.

Woman: Yes! Justice is a source of comfort.

Director: Would you say justice is a mental comfort?

Woman: Also a spiritual comfort.

Director: And it leads to physical comfort.

Woman: How so?

Director: Getting justice may make stress, anxiety, shortness of breath, headaches all go away. No?

Woman: That's true.

Director: Can we go so far as to say that mental or spiritual discomfort causes physical discomfort?

Woman: We certainly can.

Director: And what of the other way round?

Woman: Physical discomfort causing mental discomfort? I think it does, when it's severe or prolonged.

SPIRIT, EXCITEMENT

Director: But you dropped mention of spiritual discomfort. Why?

Woman: Our spirit should be stronger than that.

Director: You really don't think severe, prolonged discomfort can break our spirit?

Woman: I do. But I don't like to dwell on the fact. There's something tragically sad about the thing.

Director: But we agree that when we lend someone comfort, we should bring not just spiritual comfort, but physical comfort as well?

Woman: That's why we bring food to funerals. But maybe I shouldn't have mentioned funerals.

Director: Tell me. Aside from justice, what other sorts of spiritual comfort are there?

Woman: Well, the greatest comfort of all is love.

Director: Loving or being loved?

Woman: Both.

Director: Reciprocated love.

Woman: Exactly.

Director: You know, some say one always loves more than the other.

Woman: They say lots of foolish things. Fully reciprocated love is hard.

Director: How so?

Woman: You must work at it constantly.

Director: You always adjust to meet the other where they are?

Woman: And they always adjust to meet us where we are.

Director: But if we're both moving that way, where are we?

Woman: In heavenly bliss.

Director: You have that with your friend.

Woman: I do. And I pray she's doing alright in there now. And I say a prayer for your friend, too. I truly hope he'll come out of this well.

Director: So do I. I would miss him very much.

Woman: Tell me about him.

Director: He's awkward and full of life. Eager to learn new things. Serious, often enough. Charming when he speaks, without meaning to be. Mostly without guile. Handsome, but not overly so. In all? A friend. How about your friend?

Woman: Bright like the clear blue sky. Hopeful in all good things. Sometimes down, but never for long. Modest, but with a backbone of pride. Beautiful, in a pretty sort of way.

Director: If they get out of here, we should set them up.

Woman: Maybe the four of us can have dinner some time.

Director: Will it be a comfort fest?

Woman: It will be what it will be.

Director: Is excitement comfort?

Woman: What do you mean?

Director: Are we comfortable when we're excited? You know what I mean.

Woman: Alright. I think excitement is a kind of comfort.

Director: That changes our understanding of comfort, no?

Woman: I don't see why it should.

Director: Comfort seems passive. Excitement seems active. What do you think?

Woman: You want me to choose excitement over comfort.

Director: Don't we all?

Woman: No. Some people are afraid of excitement.

Director: Why would they be?

Woman: All excitement involves risk.

Director: Unlike comfort?

Woman: Comfort involves no risk.

Director: Why?

Woman: It's in the nature of things.

Relaxed yet Alert

Director: Comfort involves no risk? Not even in what we think?

Woman: You're talking about taking comfort in a lie.

Director: Yes. Don't you think that happens?

Woman: It does.

Director: But it's a sickly sort of comfort.

Woman: Are the sick ever really comfortable?

Director: I was once sick in the dead of winter with terrible chills. My family moved our living room couch right in front of the roaring fireplace and set me there.

Woman: You were comfortable?

Director: Comfortable enough to die.

Woman: Should we be comfortable as we die? Or maybe I shouldn't speak of this now.

Director: I don't know. Can we be comfortable and afraid?

Woman: That's a strange question. I was once flying in first class, very comfortable indeed. We hit terrible turbulence. I was afraid I'd die. My comfort vanished at once.

Director: So what are we saying? Fear and comfort don't mix?

Woman: I don't see how they can.

Director: But when we're afraid, physical comforts help.

Woman: Give an example.

Director: When I was a boy, I was sometimes afraid I'd be beaten up. Others came to stand by my side. Their physical presence comforted me, and made me less afraid.

Woman: You're confusing cause and effect. You were more comfortable because you were less afraid; not less afraid because you were more comfortable.

Director: Who can say about these things? Do you think your friend would be less afraid if you were in the operating room with her?

Woman: I... don't know. Do you?

Director: My friend knows I know nothing about surgery. I don't think I would comfort him.

Woman: Not even if you were standing back on the edge of the room?

Director: I honestly don't know. He might see me as a distraction.

Woman: For him?

Director: For the doctors at work.

Woman: I see. I think you have a point. Do the doctors need to be comfortable when they work?

Director: Hmm. They should be confident, though cautious. Maybe we should ask it the other way round. Should they be uncomfortable?

Woman: No, because that might cause them to make mistakes. But not too comfortable, for the same reason.

Director: Just comfortable enough.

Woman: Relaxed yet alert.

Director: That sounds like a good way to be in life.

Woman: Yes. Most people, when they relax, get drowsy.

Director: I have a friend who comes home from grueling work, relaxes, then writes. Can't be drowsy for that.

Woman: That's what I do!

Director: What do you write?

Woman: Children's stories.

Director: Who does the drawing?

Woman: I do.

Director: You do both? That's impressive. I always thought the model was that one person did the story and another drew it up.

Woman: That's often how it is—but not with me.

Conversations

Director: Are you comfortable when you work on your books?

Woman: Always. I change into comfortable clothes, turn down the lights, light a candle, fix a very nice cup of tea, and set to. Do you have anything like this in your life?

Director: I write on occasion.

Woman: What do you write?

Director: Philosophy, mainly.

Woman: Oh, I never liked philosophy.

Director: Why not?

Woman: Tell you what. Why don't you say what you like about it, and maybe I'll learn to come around?

Director: Fair enough. I write essays at times. But mostly I write conversations.

Woman: Conversations you've had?

Director: I did that once. I had a conversation with a philosopher one evening over coffee. It made a very strong impression on me. When I got home I wrote it down, all that I could remember.

Woman: Do you look at it often?

Director: No.

Woman: Why not? It sounds like a wonderful thing!

Director: I burned it the very next day.

Woman: Oh, why would you do such a thing!

Director: I didn't want anyone else ever to find it.

Woman: But why? What could be so terrible if discovered?

Director: It was the key to philosophy.

Woman: A secret key? Excuse me for smiling. You sound like a little boy! What's the key?

Director: It's a secret.

Woman: Ha! I know what you're doing. You're trying to take my mind off my friend.

Director: I am. But there really is a key. Why don't you try to guess?

Woman: Alright. You have to love knowledge or wisdom or whatever—with all your heart.

Director: You're on to something there.

Woman: Is it the knowledge?

Director: Yes, but that's no secret.

Woman: And it's the same with the wisdom?

Director: Yes.

Woman: Then it must be the 'whatever'!

Director: Correct.

Woman: So what is whatever?

Director: If you have to ask, you'll never know.

TEASING

Woman: Oh, now you're just being a tease.

Director: Well, let me give you a hint. If you could do whatever you want to do, what would it be?

Woman: I'd spend time with my friend. And you?

Director: I would do 'whatever'. And whatever would involve a friend.

Woman: You'd talk?

Director: Yes.

Woman: You'd talk philosophy.

Director: I would.

Woman: So the secret key to philosophy is to talk philosophy.

Director: Any time you can.

Woman: That's not such a terribly good secret.

Director: The secret involves knowing when you *can* talk philosophy.

Woman: How can you know?

Director: You have to tease a bit in order to find out.

Woman: Why not just be direct?

Director: Do you remember what happened to Socrates?

Woman: He was put to death for philosophizing.

Director: Socrates was sometimes direct.

Woman: So if he had only been smart like you he would have lived and philosophized on?

Director: Well, he was old when they put him to death.

Woman: Let me see if I understand. You tease a bit in order to see if someone is receptive and unlikely to take offense.

Director: Precisely.

Woman: Why take offense with philosophy?

Director: Because it might make you very... uncomfortable.

Woman: How, Director?

Director: Have you ever heard someone preface a question with, 'Do you mind if I ask you a personal question?'

Woman: Of course.

Director: Philosophy is all about personal things.

Woman: That can't be true. I've read Kant and Hegel. They weren't talking about personal things.

Director: Reason and History? Nothing more personal.

Woman: How do you figure?

Director: Reason is how we think; how we think is, largely, who we are. History is, largely, how we orient ourselves in the world; our orientation is who we are. Personal.

Woman: Alright, I'll take your point. So what will you do now? Tease me about what I think of World War II?

Director: The topic of teasing has to come up naturally.

Woman: It just did.

Director: You really want to talk about World War II?

Woman: Not really. I really want to talk about tease, in the sense of temptation.

Director: Ah, you understand.

Woman: Of course I do. It's not about making fun of someone. It's about temptation. Tease enough people like that and I bet they put you to death.

Director: It depends on the topic.

Woman: You're talking about taboos?

Director: Sure, taboos can be the topic. But more often than not, they're not.

Woman: Then what's the topic?

Director: It has to do with strongly held beliefs.

BELIEF

Woman: Can you give an example?

Director: Well, since it came up—there was a time when you couldn't admit the heroic role played by the Soviets in the Second World War.

Woman: Meaning we might have lost without them.

Director: Maybe not lost, but not as quickly won.

Woman: The Soviets were bad, our enemy, and therefore could have done no good.

Director: That's the way it was for a long time.

Woman: But surely people knew.

Director: Some people knew, but they kept their mouths shut.

Woman: They weren't philosophers.

Director: No, they weren't.

Woman: We took all the credit.

Director: For a long time, yes.

Woman: So how would you tease about this?

Director: I'd say, 'Look! Twenty-seven million Soviets died in WWII. Five-hundred-thousand Americans died.'

Woman: But those numbers couldn't have been widely available back then.

Director: They were available but not widely known.

Woman: But this isn't really *teasing*; it's just stating the facts.

Director: We can certainly tease with facts. I'd ask next, 'What do you think of that?' And my friend might say, 'The numbers must be wrong'; or, 'We were clearly better fighters'; or you can imagine the rest.

Woman: What's the belief?

Director: I don't know. But usually when someone challenges well established facts, they are driven by some belief. Who knows? Maybe my friend's grandfather fought in WWII, and any perceived slight on the role of the United States counts as an insult to him. This is a problem because my friend believes his grandfather was the greatest man who ever lived.

Woman: These things get complicated. But who cares what your friend thinks of his grandfather? I think it's rather nice.

Director: It's not nice if he feels inferior his whole life, and looks for a fight every chance he has—in order to prove himself as great.

Woman: Well, I know that happens often enough. Philosophy really cares about things like that?

Director: Like I said—it's personal. I don't want my friend getting into stupid fights.

Woman: You're a true friend. But what are you trying to do? Stop your friend from believing in his grandfather?

Director: I'd like him to see that man as human. Nothing more; nothing less.

Woman: And that will cure his inferiority complex?

Director: It will help, but the cure comes in what my friend does next.

Woman: Some heroic non-violent deed?

Director: Yes.

Woman: Like what? Going to the library and learning the facts of World War Two?

Director: Now I think you're teasing me.

Woman: What am I tempting you toward?

Director: I don't know. I think you're teasing me in the sense of having fun.

Woman: Well, you're wrong. I do think that it takes courage to go into those library stacks all alone and search for truth. That's why it's not often done.

Director: I agree. Why do you think it's not often done?

Woman: Because unlike you, most people are afraid when they're alone.

SEARCHING

Director: But what are we talking about? Think of the thousands upon thousands of students who every day go into those stacks looking for truth.

Woman: There's all the difference here. They were told what to look for.

Director: Why does that matter?

Woman: They know it must be there. There's comfort in that knowledge.

Director: Oh.

Woman: You seem surprised.

Director: I never thought of it this way.

Woman: So I'm the philosopher to you!

Director: And I'm grateful. Yes, they know it must be there. And even if it's not, they're rewarded for reporting that fact.

Woman: But if you or I go into a library, a huge intimidating library, searching for an answer—we are very aware there may be none.

Director: And yet we search.

Woman: Yes, and if we exhaust ourselves to no avail, we take the search elsewhere—outside.

Director: I like the way you think. But I wonder about something.

Woman: What?

Director: What makes a library intimidating?

Woman: You don't know where to start.

Director: I've never understood that. You just... start.

Woman: But what if you're in the wrong place?

Director: What's the right place? It's where you choose to start.

Woman: People are afraid to set out on their own like that.

Director: Then it can't just be a problem with libraries.

Woman: No, it's not. It's a problem with life. People don't know where to start—in anything.

Director: I blame the Greeks.

Woman: What do you mean?

Director: Plato or Aristotle said, 'The beginning is half of the whole.'

Woman: I think it's true.

Director: Well, it's not very helpful for people who are afraid to begin.

Woman: So what would you tell them?

Director: Don't be afraid of the whole—because it doesn't exist.

Woman: Do you say this because people believe in the whole?

Director: They do. The truth is that there is no whole, just a constantly evolving thing.

Woman: Is our life a constantly evolving thing and nothing more?

Director: Maybe not nothing more, but yes.

Woman: What more might it be?

Director: It becomes more when a snapshot is taken. This snapshot is usually what people think of as the whole.

Woman: But it's a sort of lie?

Director: It is. Sometimes I think photography, and the metaphors it's spawned, has hurt more than helped.

Woman: The camera steals your soul.

Director: Maybe there's some truth in that. We're all playing for that shot.

Woman: You're not.

Director: I'm not always so sure. When I search, what am I searching for?

Woman: Answers.

Director: To what?

Woman: The problems you face.

Director: What if one of my problems is fame.

Woman: I don't understand.

Director: What if I want to be famous?

Woman: We all want to be famous.

Director: I'd like to understand why.

FAME

Woman: What's the problem with fame?

Director: I think we first need to address a simple fact.

Woman: What fact?

Director: There are two types of desire for fame. One, we want to be known for what we want to be known. Two, we want to be known for what we are.

Woman: Yes, but three—we want both.

Director: One involves a sort of mask. Two involves no mask. Three involves both mask and no mask at once? How is that possible?

Woman: Three means most people will see the mask and only the mask. But we leave clues for the few to see us as we are.

Director: So what's the problem with fame?

Woman: Do you agree that three is the best way to go?

Director: I do.

Woman: Then the problem is, as it is with one, that we believe we really are our mask.

Director: Or masks.

Woman: Yes.

Director: What's wrong with that?

Woman: We lose touch with who we are.

Director: What if it's more comfortable that way?

Woman: We're not comfortable with ourselves?

Director: I think that many aren't. And I think there's a widespread belief that we *ought* to be comfortable with ourselves.

Woman: Shouldn't we?

Director: I don't know. This strikes me as a modern belief. I'm not sure it was always thought of this way.

Woman: Isn't it the better belief?

Director: Maybe we ought to make more of ourselves than we are. And then we can feel comfortable with all we've achieved.

Woman: Well, I see what you mean—though I don't know I agree.

Director: Are you opposed to achievement?

Woman: What a question to ask. So what if I am?

Director: So, you'd strike me as a remarkable person.

Woman: People think it's wrong to think that way.

Director: Do they think it's wrong to say this? 'I don't want to achieve anything. I just want to be what I am.'

Woman: It's funny, but putting it that way makes it seem less bad.

Director: Why?

Woman: Because most people believe you should just be what you are.

Director: But they still have a problem with not achieving anything.

Woman: The ambitious would. 'What I am is ambitious—and I will conquer the world.'

CONQUERING

Director: Do the ambitious derive comfort from conquering the world?

Woman: I think they derive relief.

Director: Can you say more?

Woman: The ambitious experience their ambition as a sort of duress. Then when they achieve something notable, they feel relief.

Director: Long lasting relief?

Woman: Fleeting relief.

Director: But was 'duress' really the right choice of word? It implies you're doing something against your will.

Woman: And the ambitious will their success. Maybe they're willing against their nature.

Director: Ambition isn't ambition by nature?

Woman: Well, let's think about it. Have you ever known someone who was ambitious, but wasn't always that way?

Director: That's an excellent question. I've known people who've learned to apply themselves. I've known people who learned better how to succeed. But to learn to be ambitious? That strikes me as rare.

Woman: I agree.

Director: Then how could they will against their will?

Woman: Something affects them when they're very young.

Director: How young?

Woman: Maybe in the womb.

Director: That's pretty young. But what are you saying? No one by nature wants to be ambitious? It's the result of some outside force?

Woman: Yes.

Director: Hmm. And this force robs them of the comfort of the womb?

Woman: Yes. And they spend the rest of their lives trying to get that comfort back.

Director: And they think achievement is the key. And it is, for a fleeting moment.

Woman: It's why some people work for years and years to achieve, and they are rewarded with a moment of satisfaction.

Director: Oh, but that can't be true. Their achievement might open the door to other comforts—friends, a job, fame, whatever.

Woman: True, but maybe it doesn't.

Director: Then it would be best to nip ambition in the bud.

Woman: Yes, though that somehow sounds wrong.

Director: That's because we encourage ambition. But that wasn't always so. Ambition used to be bad.

Woman: In a static society, sure.

Director: The opposite of what we have today?

Woman: If our society isn't dynamic, I don't know what society ever was.

Director: What makes it dynamic?

Woman: People can move around.

Director: Literally and figuratively?

Woman: Yes. Up and down and all around.

Director: Do they move to where they'll be most comfortable?

Woman: I don't know.

Director: Why wouldn't they?

Woman: I think people *stay* where they're comfortable. But do they move there? How can they tell?

Director: Tell where they'll be comfortable? Oh, I think there are signs.

Woman: Are you comfortable where you are now?

Director: At my job? There are things I take comfort in. But overall? No.

Woman: Why don't you find another job?

Director: I keep my eyes open; but I haven't seen anything that looks like comfort.

Woman: Well, work *is* work after all. No one pays you to sit on your couch in your pajamas and relax.

RELAXATION

Director: Is that your idea of comfort?

Woman: It's my idea of relaxation.

Director: Can we be uncomfortable while we relax?

Woman: I think it's easier to ask if we can relax while we're uncomfortable—and we can.

Director: Can you give an example?

Woman: Suppose you're hard at work on your feet all day. The shoes you're wearing are too tight. When you finally sit down your feet still hurt, but despite that discomfort you're able to relax.

Director: Would you say your feet are relaxed?

Woman: Sure.

Director: How do you know?

Woman: They feel better.

Director: And that's what relaxation is, feeling better?

Woman: You're a funny one. Don't you think that's what it is?

Director: I'm not sure. Sometimes I feel better when I get off the couch and go for a run.

Woman: Do you feel better while you're running, or after the run?

Director: Both. Am I relaxed while I run?

Woman: I would say you are. After all, running can take away stress.

Director: Countering stress is what relaxation is for. The foot felt stress all day.

Woman: And you felt stress on the couch.

Director: What sort of stress do you think I felt?

Woman: Who knows? We all have worries. You need to get out and get your mind off them.

Director: I think when I run.

Woman: Good. Thinking and obsessing are different things.

Director: How do you know I obsess about my worries?

Woman: You strike me as the type.

Director: Would you say I'm comforted by my run?

Woman: If it stops the obsessing, yes.

Director: If one of my stressors is that I have a lot to do for work, am I comforted when I start working on that work?

Woman: You are.

Director: So I can say I'm most comfortable while I'm at work.

Woman: What do we say for the poor people who don't feel stress from piled up work?

Director: They're comfortable not doing their work. I don't think there's anything else we can say for them.

Woman: Have we hit on the secret to success?

Director: Maybe we have. You have to be relaxed when you work. You have to want that relaxation. You have to want to work. You look forward to work. And no one can tear you away.

Woman: Ha, ha!

Director: Why are you laughing?

Woman: Because it's ridiculous! That's why.

Director: But why is it ridiculous?

Woman: I don't care how much you love your work. You will get tired. And when you get tired you'll want to stop. And then you'll relax.

Director: How fortunate. You're relaxed all the time, both when you work and when you stop.

Woman: I guess some people have all the luck.

YOURSELF

Director: I think such people are comfortable with themselves.

Woman: I think that's true. If you're not, how can you ever relax?

Director: I suppose you'd have to wear yourself out.

Woman: Yes, and then you don't relax—you collapse.

Director: But if you keep that up, you'll likely become unwell.

Woman: Oh, I agree. That's why I think most people have to be at least a little bit comfortable with themselves. It's not an all or nothing thing.

Director: I imagine someone who is wholly uncomfortable with themselves might oscillate between that and being wholly comfortable.

Woman: That sounds like some kind of disorder.

Director: Maybe it's not so uncommon. Many of us have something we love to do, no?

Woman: Of course.

Director: Are we comfortable when we do what we love?

Woman: I would think so. And it's weird in a way. We lose ourselves when we do what we love. And yet that's when we're most completely ourselves.

Director: Do you think we're most ourselves when we're in comfort?

Woman: We're most ourselves when we do what we love.

Director: Can we do what we love without comfort?

Woman: Yes.

Director: You sound so sure. An example?

Woman: I love to play the violin. Can I play it, and play it well, when in discomfort? Yes, of course. What do you love to do?

Director: I love to have conversations like this.

Woman: Well, that raises an interesting question. Are you comfortable here, waiting in this room, waiting for news of your friend?

Director: Are you?

Woman: Talking to you helps. But no, I'm not comfortable here.

Director: Good news from the surgeon would help you relax?

Woman: Yes.

Director: Well, it would no doubt help me, too. And yet I'm still doing what I love. It's who I am.

Woman: I've all but told you I'm a professional violinist. What are you?

Director: As a profession? I lead a team of consultants.

Woman: Do you love it?

Director: No, but it's not so bad.

Woman: What are you via what you love?

Director: A philosopher.

Woman: Philosophers love to talk.

Director: You say that with a smile. So I'm sorry to say it's not quite true.

Woman: What do they love to do?

Director: Philosophize.

Woman: What does that mean?

Director: That's one of the questions philosophy asks.

Woman: Is it the answer to that the *key*?

Director: Yes.

Woman: Hmm. Are you philosophizing here with me?

Director: I'm not quite sure.

Woman: Why not?

Director: I might be distracted from my task.

Woman: By what?

Director: My anxiety for my friend, and sympathy with you for yours.

Woman: Oh, of course. But if we met under different circumstances?

Director: Who can say?

PHILOSOPHY

Woman: What would you ask me if we were somewhere else?

Director: I'd be lying if I said I know.

Woman: Is philosophy so situational?

Director: Philosophy is about the is.

Woman: How clever. I thought philosophy is about the ought.

Director: Philosophy concerns itself with the ought. But it's not all about the ought. But I know you can understand that.

Woman: How on earth do you know?

Director: Because music is about both the ought and is.

Woman: That's very true. Are you a musician?

Director: No, but I've made a study of musicians.

Woman: How funny. I thought you were going to say you've made a study of music.

Director: Forgive me if I say—what's there to study?

Woman: Haven't you ever wanted to make or appreciate music?

Director: I whistle and hum and drum my fingers when I want to make. I'm quite accomplished in this. And I do appreciate music—for what it is.

Woman: You sound like you don't have a very high opinion of music.

Director: Music is a wonderful thing. I mean that in the full sense of the word. But today it gets more credit than its due.

Woman: You don't like that music takes us away?

Director: Some of us never come back.

Woman: So we live a dream. Is that so bad?

Director: I don't know. I guess it depends on the dream.

Woman: You surprise me. I thought philosophers want to wake people up.

Director: If your dream is good, there is no waking you up.

Woman: But you would try?

Director: I have tried, and learned there is no waking them up. I don't waste my time.

Woman: So you only wake up those who have bad dreams?

Director: It can be really hard to wake a dreamer from a bad dream.

Woman: Then whom do you wake?

Director: Those with a mixture of good and bad.

Woman: But we all have a mixture of good and bad when we dream.

Director: I talk to those that are closely balanced.

Woman: They could go either way.

Director: Yes.

Woman: And you want them to be good. Oh, wait! You want to make that good go away! You want to wake them up!

Director: Can't we take the good from our dreams and make it real?

Woman: Well, that would be ideal —sure. And that's what philosophy does?

Director: Well....

Woman: What? Why do you hesitate?

Director: 'Good' means different things to different people.

Woman: Every word means different things to different people.

Director: An excellent point. But 'good' is especially problematic.

Woman: How so? I dream about being a good violinist; in real life I become a good violinist. No problem.

Director: What if you dream about being a good violinist, but in real life you're a terrible violinist—and there's nothing you can do. Problem?

Woman: I suppose that is a problem. You think this happens for all sorts of things?

Director: I do. But that's not really the problem I'm getting at. I'm thinking of 'good' as a moral phenomenon.

Good

Woman: Tell the truth, don't steal, respect others? That sort of thing? How is that a problem?

Director: Certain people don't deserve the truth. Do you agree?

Woman: I agree—especially the truth about us. And I suppose it follows that these people don't deserve our respect.

Director: Yes.

Woman: But what about stealing?

Director: Let me answer you with a story. I once knew a woman who lived next door to a person who had a cat. This person abused the cat. One day when he wasn't home, the woman broke in and stole the cat, and made it her own. She showered it with love and care. Was it good to steal the cat?

Woman: Absolutely. I take your point.

Director: Now let's suppose she felt guilt, guilt that made her uncomfortable all the time. Would we do well to comfort her?

Woman: Yes. But I don't think she'd feel guilt.

Director: Maybe not. But can you imagine a similar situation in which someone might?

Woman: Yes. But to me it seems more likely someone would feel guilt about lying or not respecting someone.

Director: Why?

Woman: The wellbeing of another isn't always at stake. If it were, the choice is clear.

Director: Here's the thing. I want people to lie when it's for their own wellbeing. I want them to withhold respect when it's for their own well-being. Am I bad?

Woman: You might be. Give an example of a lie.

Director: The man who abused the cat confronts the woman who stole it. He asks her if she took it. She lies and says no.

Woman: Yes, yes —no doubt about that. But that's for the wellbeing of the cat. I want to hear about a lie that involves the wellbeing of the liar.

Director: You don't think her wellbeing is at stake?

Woman: Yes, but not hers alone. I want to hear about someone's wellbeing alone.

Director: Suppose we live in an awful dystopia. The police question everyone about having gay friends. You have gay friends. If the police find this out, you go to jail—even without proof, without naming the friends. Your word is enough. Is it good to lie?

Woman: Of course it is. So philosophers teach the exceptions to the rules. They make people comfortable with them.

Director: When warranted. But what do you say? Should we examine the respect we give to others?

Woman: We certainly have the time.

Director: What does it mean to respect another?

Woman: To grant them a certain amount of dignity.

Director: Does the cat abuser deserve to be treated with dignity?

Woman: No, certainly not.

Director: Why not?

Woman: He didn't treat the cat with the respect it deserved, to put it mildly.

Director: Those who don't respect don't deserve respect.

Woman: Exactly.

Director: And if you don't deserve respect, you might deserve a lie.

Woman: That's right.

Director: And if you have something that doesn't rightly belong to you, you might deserve to have it taken away.

Woman: This is all true. And it goes to easing the conscience of the one in question, the one who might be obliged not to be 'good'.

Director: Yes.

Woman: So that's what philosophy does? It eases the conscience?

Director: That's one of the things it does, where appropriate.

Woman: What else does it do?

Ice

Director: It breaks the ice.

Woman: As we've broken the ice today.

Director: I like that you said 'we'. Because no one alone can break the ice.

Woman: That's true. But I have to admit. My fear for my friend is starting to chill me again.

Director: Philosophy might be able to help.

Woman: How? It warms us up when we're cold?

Director: And cools us down when we're hot.

Woman: So philosophy is a sort of doctor of the soul?

Director: It can be.

Woman: But that's a problem.

Director: How so?

Woman: What if I read a book meant to cool us down when I'm cold? Or the other way round.

Director: That's why philosophy is best in person.

Woman: So the philosopher can tell what you need.

Director: Right.

Woman: Well, I'm telling you I need to warm up. What do you say?

Director: We need to find what's making you cold.

Woman: But we know that already—fear for my friend.

Director: You fear your friend will die.

Woman: Yes, I do. And now what will you tell me? That death isn't the end? Haven't a million philosophers taught us that?

Director: Well, I have no intention of being one-million-and-one.

Woman: What will you teach? Or will you just try to get my mind off things.

Director: I'd rather get your mind off things than teach.

Woman: You don't need to be a philosopher to do that. A clown might succeed where you might fail.

Director: Should I turn on the television and look for clowns?

Woman: No. I hate the television in places like this.

Director: Why do you hate it?

Woman: Because it's meant to be a distraction. And it doesn't distract—it annoys.

Director: Isn't annoyance a sort of distraction?

Woman: Maybe I don't want to be distracted.

Director: You want to focus on your fear—and heat yourself up.

Woman: Yes.

Director: How can you heat yourself up?

Woman: Right now I'm so cold I can't even cry.

Director: Crying would be better.

Woman: Infinitely so, yes.

Director: What would make you cry?

Woman: Thinking of the all the good things about my friend.

Director: What's one of the good things?

Woman: Her laugh. It's so bright and strong.

Director: Does she laugh often?

Woman: No, only now and then. That's how I know it's true. How about your friend? Does he laugh often?

Director: Sometimes his laughter is true; often it's fake.

Woman: Oh. I'm sorry.

Director: It's okay. We're working on it.

LAUGHTER 2

Woman: How can you work on laughter?

Director: When I think his laughter is fake, I ask him what's so funny. And then we have a conversation on this.

Woman: What do you two conclude?

Director: Usually? That it wasn't funny.

Woman: That it made him nervous?

Director: Yes. It made him uncomfortable.

Woman: We hope that laughter brings us comfort.

Director: We do. But this less-than-genuine laughter can be a great help.

Woman: It's a sort of diagnostic tool.

Director: Yes, just so.

Woman: And we want to find the thing that makes us uncomfortable and bring comfort to it.

Director: In a sense.

Woman: In a sense?

Director: At heart the problem is often a false belief, a being false to oneself.

Woman: The false belief is a sort of funny bone here?

Director: That puts it well.

Woman: So you get rid of the false belief and become true to yourself. Then you'll laugh like my friend.

Director: That's the hope.

Woman: Why is it only a hope?

Director: If the belief is like a bone, a funny bone as you said, it has to be replaced.

Woman: By becoming true to yourself.

Director: Yes.

Woman: Being true to yourself lends structure and support, like a bone.

Director: If our metaphor is right, yes.

Woman: But there are bones and then there are bones.

Director: You see the problem.

Woman: If it's a little finger bone, it's one thing; if it's your skull.... What do you do if it's the skull?

Director: There are a lot of broken bones in this world. It takes triage at times.

Woman: At times? I would think it's necessary *all* the time. How do you decide?

Director: I decide what's best for me.

Woman: What? You can't mean that.

Director: But I do.

Woman: That's so... so... selfish! Ha!

Director: I made you laugh again. Why did you laugh?

Woman: Because what you said is outrageous but true!

Director: That's a good reason to laugh.

Woman: You don't mind being laughed at?

Director: Not when it's a laugh like this.

Woman: So how do you decide?

Director: I give priority to friends and potential friends.

Woman: Potential friends. Interesting. You size people up?

Director: I certainly do. And then I decide if I'd like to be friends with them.

Woman: Most people just stumble into their friends.

Director: And most people don't laugh true.

FRIENDS

Woman: Let's say you rate a potential friend on a scale of one to ten, ten being most desirable. If you encounter someone who's a ten, and they have a broken arm, it's an easy choice.

Director: Of course.

Woman: But if you encounter someone who's a six and has a broken head?

Director: It's a harder choice.

Woman: So how do you choose?

Director: I have to weigh what else is going on in my life.

Woman: You see whether you have what it takes.

Director: Right. But here the metaphor falls short. When you get into it, you really have no way of knowing exactly what it will take. Something could seem minor but turn out to be a very large problem indeed.

Woman: Yes, of course—that makes sense. But don't you learn as you go? Can't you get better at estimating what it will take?

Director: If all the problems remained the same, sure, I could learn. But the world changes even under our feet. New problems arise, never before seen. How do you estimate that?

Woman: So what do you do?

Director: I have to be willing either to see it all the way through, no matter what, or break things off.

Woman: What makes you want to see it through?

Director: Love.

Woman: And break things off? Lack of love?

Director: Sometimes.

Woman: I don't understand. Are you saying sometimes you break it off when you love?

Director: Yes, and it's the hardest thing I've ever done.

Woman: Why did you break it off?

Director: Because both of us knew—and I mean *knew*—what the problem was.

Woman: And they needed to fix it by themselves.

Director: Sometimes there's no other way.

Woman: Why? Why not fix it for them?

Director: There are two reasons. One, I don't know how. Two, even if I did—they'll have more respect for themselves if they do it on their own. But it's funny.

Woman: What's funny?

Director: Are you still feeling cold?

Woman: I'm not. How did this happen?

Director: You love your friend and can relate to what we've said. That's enough to warm anyone up.

Woman: I think you're right. But how do you think I relate?

Director: Maybe your friend plays the role of me in what we've said?

Woman: We play that role, the doctor, to each other. That's how it should be. But how would your friend feel if he heard you calling yourself his doctor?

Director: He would feel good—because I often fall and break my head. He'd be glad to acknowledge that his services to me are returned.

Woman: When was the last time you broke your head?

Director: I fell in love and acted the fool.

Woman: What did you do?

Director: I talked about it incessantly.

Woman: And your friend intervened?

Director: Yes, he told me to stop acting the fool.

Woman: And that was enough?

Director: Oh, no. It took my falling and breaking my head.

Woman: Then how did your friend help?

Director: As soon as I felt the crack, I knew he had been right. And so I saw the way to start healing again.

Woman: Again. This really happens often with you?

Director: Not as much as it used to, but often enough.

Woman: Why don't you learn?

Director: Maybe I haven't found the right teacher yet.

FLIRTING

Woman: Director, are you flirting with me?

Director: Woman, you're no teacher.

Woman: How do you know?

Director: I think you fall and crack your head often, too.

Woman: Well, I'll tell you—it's true. My friend tells me when I act the fool.

Director: Do you listen?

Woman: Not until it's too late.

Director: Yes, this is the problem.

Woman: What do you mean?

Director: Listening. Philosophy has a problem here.

Woman: Oh, we're back to philosophy now?

Director: I'm always back to philosophy, however far I stray.

Woman: What's the problem with listening?

Director: A philosopher has to know when to listen and when not to listen.

Woman: Let me guess. A philosopher refuses to listen to comforting words.

Director: How did you know?

Woman: Because it's the opposite of when most people listen. *You* listen especially well when things that make you uncomfortable are said. Why?

Director: Because I know there's something to be learned. There's something there—in it.

Woman: And you always want to be *in it*.

Director: I do.

Woman: That means there's no time for love.

Director: Wrong. That means there's no time for a *relationship*.

Woman: What's wrong with a relationship?

Director: Nothing and everything.

Woman: Tell me what that means, philosopher.

Director: We have a relationship with everything in this world. But to say we have a singular relationship, an exclusive relationship—that's to spit in the face of the rest of the world.

Woman: Oh, you're full of nonsense. I have a relationship with my dog. Does that mean I deny my 'relationships' with the rest of the canine world?

Director: I depends who you are.

Woman: Say more.

Director: I have a favorite example along these lines. I know someone who has a pet pig, and loves that pig dearly—but he still eats pork.

Woman: What? I don't understand the point.

Director: Love, exclusive love, excludes the other pigs.

Woman: I'd rather he didn't eat pork.

Director: Is that because you care about justice?

Woman: I feel sorry for the pigs. But I care about justice for human beings.

Director: If you've excluded someone, can you do justice to them?

Woman: Are you suggesting we can only do justice within our circles of love?

Director: That's how it always seems to happen, yes.

Woman: What is justice—to you?

Director: Something that doesn't have much to do with love.

JUSTICE

Woman: Tell me something. Are you more comfortable with justice or love?

Director: Love.

Woman: But love makes you break your head.

Director: And justice makes me break... my heart.

Woman: I would have thought love would break the heart.

Director: Not my kind of love.

Woman: What kind of love is yours?

Director: Pure love.

Woman: And what of pure justice?

Director: What kind of justice is pure?

Woman: I don't know. What is justice?

Director: Getting what you deserve.

Woman: You don't want what you deserve.

Director: I don't know what I deserve. So how can I trust that someone else does?

Woman: If you ask me, you deserve love—the love of a friend.

Director: Thank you. That's the highest honor I can imagine.

Woman: Do you really mean it?

Director: Well, I'm not known for my imagination.

Woman: Ha! You've made me laugh again. I want to make *you* laugh.

Director: Others have tried.

Woman: You *deserve* to laugh.

Director: Why?

Woman: Because you're honest.

Director: You don't know me well enough yet.

Woman: I think I know what I need to know.

Director: And what do you know?

Woman: I know enough.

Director: That's a good philosophical answer.

Woman: How so?

Director: Philosophers don't need to know everything.

Woman: What do they need to know?

Director: That while we don't always deserve love, sometimes it's ours.

Woman: Why do they need to know that?

Director: Because anyone who thinks they deserve love...

Woman: ...doesn't.

Director: What does someone like that deserve?

Woman: I don't know.

Director: Does that make you unjust?

Woman: I really don't care. It makes me true.

Director: Truth and justice can be opposed?

Woman: Like love and hate.

Director: Well, I'm impressed.

Woman: That I can hate?

Director: That justice isn't your all.

Woman: What of those for whom justice is all?

Director: What's to say? They're monstrous.

MONSTERS

Woman: But we need justice.

Director: Why?

Woman: Everyone wants to get what they deserve!

Director: Bad people do?

Woman: Well....

Director: Who really wants what they deserve?

Woman: The good.

Director: How do they know they're good?

Woman: Their philosopher friends tell them.

Director: I told my friend, the one they're operating on now, he has *some* good in him.

Woman: Then you're a rotten man.

Director: Should I have told him he's *wholly* good?

Woman: Before his surgery? Yes!

Director: Is that what you told *your* friend?

Woman: I told her this, to bolster her.

Director: And?

Woman: She... denied it.

Director: Then laughed.

Woman: How did you know!

Director: If someone told me I were wholly good, I too would laugh.

Woman: Why?

Director: Because I'd know they were lying out of love.

Woman: Is that so bad?

Director: It's monstrous.

Woman: No, you don't mean it. It's an innocent mistake.

Director: Perhaps. But it's an offer of false comfort, nonetheless.

Woman: Why do I get the impression you'd prefer if no one offered comfort at all?

Director: That's the best comfort there is.

Woman: A paradox—something philosophers love.

Director: Don't you think the truth is a comfort to some?

Woman: Maybe. But what are we saying? If you take comfort in comfort you're weak; and if you take comfort in *no comfort* you're strong?

Director: Why do you say the truth is no comfort?

Woman: To tell you the truth—I'm no longer sure what we're saying!

Director: There's no greater comfort than in long suppressed truth.

Woman: What? What does that mean? I would think suppressing truth is decidedly *uncomfortable!*

Director: Maybe at first. But over time? We can grow comfortable with that.

Woman: I think you're being sarcastic. But what if?

Director: What if what?

Woman: What if the truth in question is bad?

Director: What truth is bad?

Woman: Can you really think that way?

Director: Tell a truth that's bad.

Woman: As you go into surgery, I lean close and say, 'You're a philandering liar, and I hope you come out of it well.' Comfort?

Director: Am I really a liar?

Woman: Oh, stop. You know what I mean.

Director: You're saying if the truth spoken is generally considered bad, you can't take comfort in that.

Woman: Of course.

Director: But you can—if it's really the truth.

Woman: How?

Director: It has to do with honesty.

Woman: Redemption?

Director: There's something to that.

REDEMPTION

Woman: You assume we're redeemed by simply acknowledging the truth.

Director: No, it takes more than that.

Woman: What does it take?

Director: Acceptance.

Woman: What if you accept it before someone confronts you with it?

Director: You're already redeemed.

Woman: Oh, that's nonsense—and you know it.

Director: Why?

Woman: If you're already redeemed, what stops you from covering it up the rest of your life?

Director: Nothing. Or, everything.

Woman: Let me guess. The truth screams within to come out.

Director: Of course. Who wants screaming inside?

Woman: We want to share our truth.

Director: Very badly. Sometimes we can; sometimes we can't.

Woman: Tell me a truth about you.

Director: I really love nothing more than conversations like this.

Woman: That's not bad.

Director: Imagine you and I were in a relationship. Then imagine that every time I'm away you suspect I'm having conversations like this. How would that sit with you?

Woman: Are you saying the conversation we're having today isn't special and unique?

Director: It is special and unique. But I have special and unique conversations whenever I can.

Woman: This has to do with love.

Director: It does. Nothing fuels conversation like love.

Woman: Well, then I would be upset.

Director: Can you think of someone who wouldn't?

Woman: I can—you!

Director: You assume I would be in a relationship with someone like me.

Woman: Wouldn't you?

Director: I know better.

Woman: So what are you saying? Like isn't attracted to like?

Director: No, like *is* attracted to like. But identical and identical don't mix.

Woman: Oh, no one is *identical* to another in this world.

Director: Close enough is good enough for me.

Woman: I think I would like an identical to share my life with me.

Director: An identical what?

Woman: What do you mean?

Director: What are you so that we can know what your identical is?

Woman: I'm... I'm... a caring and sensitive woman! What are you?

Director: A philosopher.

Woman: Philosophers can't be with one another?

Director: They can't.

Woman: Can't or won't?

Director: What's the difference?

Woman: One is an impossibility; the other is a matter of will.

Director: For a true philosopher going against will *is* an impossibility.

Woman: But what will? Not to take comfort in one another?

Director: I'd better explain what I mean by will.

Will

Woman: What's to explain? Everyone knows what will is.

Director: What is it?

Woman: Holding firm to get what you want. So what are you saying? Philosophers always get what they want?

Director: Ha, ha. No, I'm not sure I'd say that. Unless....

Woman: Unless what?

Director: Unless the philosopher is a sort of fatalist.

Woman: What would that mean?

Director: He—

Woman: Or she.

Director: —embraces every chance that comes his way.

Woman: No resistance to anything?

Director: None. Can you imagine two people like that in a relationship?

Woman: That would be... a catastrophe. In fact, it's a catastrophe if only one person in the relationship is that way.

Director: I agree. Fatalists are living catastrophes.

Woman: They exercise no will.

Director: No, they do. It takes an effort of will to embrace your fate.

Woman: But it's not *impossible* to resist every now and then. Is it?

Director: Forgive me, but you don't know what kind of net of causality a philosopher gets entangled in once he—

Woman: Or she.

Director: —starts. There simply is no resisting.

Woman: That sounds like a pathetic life to me. Tell me about the opposite kind of philosopher, the one who resists everything.

Director: That is an equally hard life. There is no rest.

Woman: No comfort.

Director: None—except in the very willing.

Woman: But then you're saying it's an absolute life of comfort!

Director: Just as there is absolute comfort in the embrace of fate.

Woman: So philosophers are creatures of comfort.

Director: The hedonists are, certainly. The stoics? I'm not so sure.

Woman: Is that all there are, essentially? Hedonists and stoics?

Director: There are other types. Skeptics are my favorite.

Woman: What are they like?

Director: They doubt everything—absolutely everything.

Woman: On principle?

Director: You've hit it right on the head. That's their hypocrisy. They doubt everything but the principle of doubt.

Woman: But it can take a great amount of will to doubt certain things.

Director: To sustain the doubt, yes. That's the thing. Anyone can doubt for a moment. But to doubt and hold that doubt in suspension always in your mind—that's no small feat.

Woman: But what's the point?

Director: It's an exercise of will. And there is satisfaction in that. Comfort, if you will.

Woman: A mind riddled with doubt satisfies? I can you tell you first hand—doubt doesn't have that effect.

Director: Maybe you haven't doubted enough?

Woman: Let's talk about something else.

SATISFACTION

Director: I'm surprised you didn't call me out.

Woman: What, to fight about doubt?

Director: No, for equating comfort and satisfaction.

Woman: Well, of course they're not the same.

Director: Because we can have one and not the other?

Woman: Yes.

Director: So I can be comfortable even though I'm not satisfied. And I can be satisfied though I lack comfort.

Woman: Do you see a problem here?

Director: I do. Lack of satisfaction can keep us up at night. If I'm up like that, how can I be comfortable?

Woman: Give an example.

Director: I get in a fight with someone at work. I apologize and mean it. She apologizes but I can tell she doesn't mean it. I'm not satisfied with her apology. It bothers me so much it keeps me up at night— even though I'm wearing my comfy pajamas, and am lying in my comfy bed, and so on with whatever else you might think makes for comfort.

Woman: I agree. Your lack of satisfaction makes comfort impossible.

Director: And how about the other way?

Woman: I'm not sure it works the other way. If you are satisfied with the apology, and you go home and find you have nothing to wear but itchy scratchy clothes, and your bed is lumpy and hurts your back, and so on—you're still satisfied with the apology.

Director: So if given a choice between comfort and satisfaction, I should choose satisfaction. Lack of comfort can't take it away. It's durable. But if I choose comfort, it *can* be taken away.

Woman: I think that's true. If it's true satisfaction, you'll always have it. Comfort comes and goes.

Director: Yes, but now I have a doubt.

Woman: What doubt?

Director: Satisfaction can be taken away.

Woman: How?

Director: Suppose I get my apology. I go home and savor it. But the next day at work the same fight breaks out.

Woman: People can take your satisfaction away. So what does this mean?

Director: It means we should take what we can get, when we can get it.

Woman: But you'll always choose satisfaction if given the choice, despite the fact that it might be taken away.

Director: Can you give an example?

Woman: The satisfaction of a job well done. This might mean staying late at work, where you're tired and uncomfortable. And yet you do— because you want the satisfaction of a job well done.

Director: Who chooses the opposite way?

Woman: The lazy. The effete. Those who just don't care.

Director: They just want to get home and relax in comfort.

Woman: Yes.

Director: Do you have contempt for them?

Woman: Believe it or not? No, I don't.

Director: Why not? Some of their colleagues likely do.

Woman: I don't like the culture of the driven. And these colleagues are likely perpetrators of drive.

Director: Can you say more?

Woman: If you sacrifice your comfort once too often out of drive, there's something wrong with you.

Director: A long term lack of comfort brings a change in our soul?

Woman: Yes, exactly. Something breaks.

Director: The driven are broken.

Woman: Don't you agree?

Director: I do. But there's something that resembles drive that leaves people whole.

EFFORT

Woman: I'd like to know what it is.

Director: Effort. Even the word sounds better. 'Eff'. A pleasant sound. 'Drr'. Not so pleasant.

Woman: Oh, be serious.

Director: Look at the way we use the words. 'He is driven' versus 'He puts in an effort'. The former is passive. Something not him is driving him to work. The latter suggests he is in control and chooses to work the way he does.

Woman: Okay, you're on to something here. If you put in an effort, you can know when it's time to stop. But if you're driven, you're blind to this in a way.

Director: I agree. Even the 'put in' part of the phrase suggests something good.

Woman: It does. It suggests you choose where your effort will go.

Director: I agree. But I think most people will think we're cutting it pretty thin.

Woman: There really is something to this, though, this difference between effort and drive. Drive can happen from outside your control. Effort is always only on you.

Director: At the end of a long day, which would you rather be, someone of effort or drive?

Woman: It's hard to turn off drive and relax. I choose effort, because when I'm done I stop.

Director: Is there more to this problem of drive?

Woman: It makes those around you uncomfortable—unless they're all driven, too.

Director: Let's clear something up. Can someone of effort achieve at as high a level as someone of drive?

Woman: Of course!

Director: Then why be driven?

Woman: I think some people don't have a choice.

Director: Why not?

Woman: The drive fills a hole in their soul.

Director: How do we get holes in our soul?

Woman: Oh, I don't know. Maybe there was something attached there that got ripped away and left a hole.

Director: Those with drive are damaged in some way. Those who make effort—great effort, tremendous effort, unbelievable effort—aren't.

Woman: I like what we're saying. But those with drive won't like this one bit.

Director: Some might listen and make the switch to effort.

Woman: What kind of person does it take?

Director: One with a touch of...

Woman: What?

Director: ...humility.

Woman: I can see that. But what we're saying is funny. I mean, there's all the difference in the world between effort and drive; but it's subtle distinction.

Director: The world is made up of subtle distinctions. That's where the power lies.

Woman: The rulers of this world I've known aren't very subtle.

Director: There's a pleasant ambiguity in that phrase. You knew the rulers, or you knew the world. Regardless, those rulers are missing out.

Woman: They're blind and blinkered and full of hate.

Director: Whence the hate?

Woman: I don't know. Every time I come across one of the driven they seem upset. My guess is that there's some hate in there. What's yours?

Director: Hate can fuel a drive. So can insecurity.

Woman: Fear.

Director: Yes, drive will often camouflage fear—and draw from it, too.

Woman: Can we make great effort if eaten with fear?

Director: It's very difficult. Best to address the fear, then turn to the effort clean.

CLEAN

Woman: Clean. I can't get comfortable if I'm not clean—in every sense.

Director: You can't be a pig and wallow in the mud?

Woman: Ha, ha. No, I can't. And I can't stand people who do. You don't strike me as a pig, Director.

Director: Why thank you, Woman. I understand how people keep their bodies clean, and their environs—but what about their minds?

Woman: Haven't you ever heard of a dirty mind?

Director: Of course I have. But what does it mean?

Woman: It means you couldn't hold a conversation like this if you had one.

Director: The dirt would get in the way.

Woman: Yes.

Director: But I think there are other ways to have a dirty mind.

Woman: Tell me how.

Director: At the simplest level? You don't reason on everything within your mind.

Woman: Nothing can escape the scrutiny?

Director: Nothing. But you can't do it all at once.

Woman: Say more.

Director: When you're twenty you might scrutinize one part of your mind.

Woman: And when you're forty another?

Director: Yes. The mind is a big house to clean.

Woman: I like the way you put it. What are our cleaning tools?

Director: Reason, logic, memory, but most importantly—honesty. Without honesty you can't come clean.

Woman: Maybe.

Director: Maybe?

Woman: Sometimes, for the sake of our health, Director—we need to lie to ourselves.

Director: That's a remarkable confession. Why?

Woman: Sometimes truth is more than we can take.

Director: So what do we do?

Woman: Isolate ourselves and save up strength.

Director: For the confrontation.

Woman: Yes.

Director: How comfortable are we when we lie to ourselves?

Woman: Not as comfortable as we are when we're clean.

Director: Does comfort have something to do with peace?

Woman: It certainly does.

Director: When we lie to ourselves, do we know at some level we're lying?

Woman: Yes, of course. It's madness—literally—to lie and not know it, at some level, for what it is.

Director: Can the mad, in this way, know peace?

Woman: No, they're tormented—always looking for the thread they lost; the thread that can take them home.

Director: The mad are never clean.

Woman: No, they're not.

Director: That's very sad. They're never comfortable. But how do you know this about madness?

Woman: I've... been mad.

Director: What happened?

Woman: The day after I won first chair I... lost my mind.

Director: And yet you're clean and healthy today. Are you comfortable with this?

Woman: Yes, mostly. But I fear a relapse.

HYGIENE

Director: That's what hygiene is for.

Woman: I don't understand.

Director: You must fight, above all else, to keep your soul clean.

Woman: I'm glad you switched from mind to soul. Was that intentional?

Director: My dear, I'm a philosopher. Everything—*everything*—I do is intentional.

Woman: Even when you play?

Director: Especially when I play.

Woman: I find that at once comforting and... frightful. Tell me, and tell me honestly, Director. Is that a blessing or a curse?

Director: Neither.

Woman: But it suggests you're completely self-aware.

Director: That's the ultimate comfort and clean.

Woman: I don't believe you. No one is completely self-aware.

Director: How do you know?

Woman: You're the one who makes me think it might be possible. And yet... I see things in you.

Director: What do you see? Lack of hygiene?

Woman: No, it's not that. It has something to do with... others.

Director: I'm not self-aware of others?

Woman: You know that's ridiculous, no. But there's something to it, none-theless.

Director: Are we dirty if we don't know others?

Woman: I think we are, in a way.

Director: Do you think I don't know others?

Woman: I think you know *certain* others.

Director: Like you?

Woman: Yes, like me.

Director: And the rest?

Woman: You get a whiff of them, and decide you want to know no more.

Director: That's part of my hygiene. I suspect they are infected. There's nothing I can learn from them other than... how to be sick.

Woman: But you already have knowledge of how to be sick.

Director: First-hand knowledge, yes.

Woman: Like me.

Director: Yes.

Woman: Somehow I take comfort in that.

Director: As do I. Why?

Woman: It takes one to know one?

Director: Ha!

Woman: I made you laugh! Does it really take one to know one?

Director: Yes, of course it does.

Woman: So you might know someone is striving and striving to be clean, even if there is still some dirt here and there.

Director: Yes, I would certainly know. And I also know—flowers only grow in dirt.

Woman: Thank you. But I assume you're talking about cultivated flowers.

Director: Wildflowers are beautiful, yes. But nothing matches the strength of the cultivated stem.

Woman: Thank you again. But the stem? Not the flower?

Director: Flowers aren't about strength. They're about beauty.

Woman: I thought you equate beauty with strength.

Director: It takes strength to stand atop that stem, fragile as beauty is.

FRAGILITY

Woman: The fragile can be strong?

Director: The fragile *have to be* strong.

Woman: Why, or else they'll face destruction?

Director: Yes, there's that. But it's also because otherwise they'll be... uncomfortable.

Woman: Strength for comfort.

Director: Yes.

Woman: That sounds... base.

Director: Tell me, Woman. Do you ever take strength in the comfort of another?

Woman: I... sometimes... do.

Director: Is that base?

Woman: Is it?

Director: No.

Woman: Do you take comfort in the strength of another?

Director: That's a very personal question.

Woman: Tell me.

Director: I do—every night when I read a philosopher.

Woman: What strength do you see?

Director: The strength to tell the truth, despite their devices.

Woman: Devices?

Director: Philosophers, despite what some of them might say, are fragile souls. They need devices to support their truth.

Woman: What's an example of a device?

Director: The trial was Socrates' device for his death.

Woman: He wanted to die?

Director: Yes. How else can you explain the crazy things he said?

Woman: But they're not crazy. They're... the foundation of Western Civilization!

Director: Is there comfort in knowing that this civilization was founded on state sponsored suicide?

Woman: Director, I really think you're talking crazy now. How about another device?

Director: Let's start with Plato. Everyone knows his *Republic*, right?

Woman: Well, the educated do.

Director: Let's focus on the educated, then. Do you remember Thrasymachus?

Woman: Not... exactly.

Director: He talks with Socrates early on in the dialogue. He argues that justice is nothing but the advantage of the strong.

Woman: And Socrates refutes him.

Director: Yes, to general applause. But how good was Socrates' argument?

Woman: Good enough to win,

Director: Precisely. This is one of Plato's devices.

Woman: I don't understand.

Director: He wants us to seriously consider Thrasymachus' point of view. But it's not *becoming* to ask someone to consider this point of view. And so he presents the view and leaves it to us.

Woman: Most will simply ignore that point of view.

Director: That's right. And those with philosophical potential... won't.

Woman: Did you consider that point of view?

Director: I did. And I rejected it.

Woman: That took strength.

Director: The argument wasn't that strong.

Woman: Don't tell me you made it as strong as it could be before rejecting it.

Director: I did.

Woman: Did that make *you* strong?

Director: To the contrary—it made me more fragile than ever.

Woman: Why fragile?

Director: Because I realized things aren't as simple as they seem.

HEARTBEATS

Woman: Socrates' arguments aren't enough.

Director: They're not. They have to be taken in context.

Woman: And you're looking for the argument that is, simply speaking, and without context—true.

Director: Here is where my heart skips a beat. No, I'm not.

Woman: I thought that's what philosophers want.

Director: Philosophers want something more.

Woman: What?

Director: To disabuse Thrasymachus of his mistake.

Woman: What was the mistake?

Director: His belief in what justice is.

Woman: So what are you saying? You don't want the simply true argument; you want the argument that heals? You want the argument that comforts the soul?

Director: My heart skips another beat.

Woman: Why? You don't want to bring comfort?

Director: To those who deserve it, yes.

Woman: Who deserves it?

Director: Those whose heart skips a beat when confronted with truth.

Woman: Why not take the truth in stride?

Director: That's the effort we make.

Woman: We? We philosophers?

Director: Of course.

Woman: Am I a philosopher?

Director: I don't know.

Woman: Be serious. Am I?

Director: Do you want to be?

Woman: No.

Director: Then you're not.

Woman: It's really that simple?

Director: We can't help wanting to be what we are.

Woman: But you know that's ridiculous. I have a nephew who wants to be a professional football player, a quarterback. The problem is—he can't throw the ball. He can't help wanting to be a quarterback; but that's not what he is.

Director: He doesn't yet know what to want.

Woman: It's really that simple for you?

Director: It's really that simple for him. He doesn't yet know what he is.

Woman: What is he? And why are you smiling?

Director: I haven't met the boy yet.

Woman: I'd like it if you did.

Director: Make the arrangements and I will come.

Woman: Thank you. He's not in much comfort, you know.

Director: Who is, when they don't know who they are?

Woman: There's comfort in this knowledge, yes?

Director: Well....

Woman: What is it?

Director: It takes something more.

PLACE

Woman: What more does it take? I thought if you *know thyself* you'll be at peace.

Director: Knowledge is a sort of beginning, and as we said that's half the whole.

Woman: What's the other half?

Director: Before we get to that, the knowledge has two parts. One, knowing who you are. Two, knowing your place.

Woman: Two follows from one.

Director: And sometimes two can teach us one.

Woman: We find where we feel good and come to know ourselves.

Director: Yes.

Woman: So what's the other half?

Director: Keeping to your place no matter what.

Woman: That's the work of a lifetime.

Director: It certainly is.

Woman: And we know we're in our place because we're comfortable there?

Director: Not... exactly. When we're not in our place we rarely find comfort. When we're in our place we do find it—but not all the time; and sometimes not often.

Woman: Then how do we know we're in our place? And why be in our place if we find no comfort there?

Director: Let's think of your nephew. Suppose he were big, fast, strong, smart—and he throws the ball like no one can. Yes, his place is to quarterback the team.

Woman: You're speaking metaphorically.

Director: I'm speaking both ways. Suppose his team is great and they win all the time. Comfort?

Woman: There's comfort in winning, yes.

Director: But now suppose he gets traded to an awful team. They lose all the time, and lose ugly. Comfort?

Woman: No, of course not.

Director: But he's still in his place? The quarterback of the team?

Woman: I... suppose. But why would they trade him?

Director: Who knows? A personality clash with the coach. Or maybe a great deal just came along. Or they have a backup quarterback who is ready and raring to go. It could be many things.

Woman: So what's the point?

Director: Sometimes being in our place is hard. Should your nephew quit football when traded to the losing team?

Woman: No.

Director: Well, imagine this for any 'place' that anyone has.

Woman: Knowing your place usually means not being too full of yourself.

Director: And it can also mean not being not full enough.

Woman: How do we know if we are?

Director: We have to test the limits of where we sit.

Woman: That's a recipe for trouble.

Director: This can be done discretely.

Woman: I don't believe it. If it's too discrete it's not a real test. Someone, somehow, will know you're testing.

Director: Then we need to make sure that this someone is on our side.

SIDES

Woman: We can't be comfortable when we're on the wrong side.

Director: In life in general?

Woman: Yes.

Director: So that includes being on the wrong side of the argument.

Woman: It does.

Director: What's the wrong side of the argument?

Woman: The preponderance of truth is on the other side.

Director: That means the other side is in the right.

Woman: Right.

Director: And when we know we're in the right, we can take comfort in that.

Woman: Of course.

Director: Even if we lose?

Woman: Then we have solace.

Director: What if we have the truth, have right—and the entire age is stacked against us? What do we do?

Woman: We fight. This is what philosophers do.

Director: How do they fight?

Woman: Some talk; some write; some do I know not what.

Director: And when people accuse philosophers of being against the spirit of the time?

Woman: What crime is there in that? Why can't people just leave philosophers alone? So what if they don't want to march in the victory parade? What harm do they do?

Director: They question the nature of the victory.

Woman: Give an example.

Director: A woman at work was named CEO after many long years of effort. We were together in the elevator one day, alone. The elevator got stuck between floors. I asked her how things were going. She said they were great. I asked her what made them great. She looked confused and annoyed. 'Revenue is up,' she said. 'That's certainly great,' I answered. There was silence for a few moments. 'You don't think that's great?' she said. 'It's great for the company,' I said. 'It might not be great for you.'

Woman: What did she say to that?

Director: She frowned, but said, 'Why not?' 'Because,' I said, 'the results were more of a relief than something that made you proud.'

Woman: You said that to her?

Director: I did.

Woman: What did she say next?

Director: 'I got your email.'

Woman: What email?

Director: I sent her a map of Dante's *Inferno* the day she was named chief.

Woman: Why would you do that? What did you say?

Director: I wrote, 'Look familiar?' I put a smiley face at the end.

Woman: You were friends with her?

Director: I only had a few interactions with her, but I got the sense she was a decent person. But she lacked a fundamental confidence in her work. I wondered why they named her chief.

Woman: Because she would go along.

Director: Yes, I think that's right. So, anyway, I asked her if she liked the map.

Woman: And?

Director: She said she threw it away.

Woman: She got angry with you?

Director: No, she simply said, 'No need for the map—I know the way by heart.'

HEART

Woman: Her heart wasn't in her work. And you knew it.

Director: Yes.

Woman: You could have had a serious conversation with her about it. Instead, you chose to make a joke of the thing with the map.

Director: What would I have done? Gotten some time on her calendar to tell her she's in the wrong place? She was gone as CEO after six months.

Woman: Her doing?

Director: In large part, yes.

Woman: Did *you* have anything to do with it?

Director: Well, I was friends with the Chief Financial Officer. He called me in one day and shut the door. He said he wanted my opinion about the CEO.

Woman: What did you tell him?

Director: That she didn't have the confidence it takes.

Woman: You betrayed her?

Director: I told him the truth. And I think I did her a favor.

Woman: So from that moment they planned to move her out.

Director: I wouldn't say it was from *that* moment. They were just looking for another weight to add to the scale.

Woman: But why take part in that... that... assassination?

Director: Her heart wasn't in the work.

Woman: Most people's hearts aren't in their work!

Director: Then we should plan more assassinations.

Woman: Okay, I know I shouldn't judge. I wasn't there. Where did she go next?

Director: I heard she became the head of a small charity having to do with service animals.

Woman: A happy ending.

Director: I'm sure she was much more comfortable there—and appreciated, too.

Woman: Appreciation is a great source of comfort.

Director: It involves knowing you for what you are and thinking what you are is good. But, of course, most of us at best get partial appreciation.

Woman: True. People often appreciate me as a violinist, but there's more to me than that. Do you believe we can ever be appreciated in full?

Director: I don't know. If so, it's rare. But I wonder about the difference between appreciation and justice.

Woman: I'm not following.

Director: You know the phrase, do full justice to someone?

Woman: Of course.

Director: What does it mean?

Woman: To describe them accurately and in full. It's usually said about someone who has a bad reputation.

Director: So we might, for instance, do full justice to Richard Nixon.

Woman: Sure, for instance.

Director: But it can also be done to someone with a good reputation.

Woman: Do full justice to Abraham Lincoln, for instance.

Director: Yes. So here's my question. Would you have be appreciated or have full justice done to you?

Woman: I'd rather be appreciated.

Director: Why?

Woman: Full justice is a scary thing! Who can stand the scrutiny of full justice?

Director: Is that why it usually comes, if it comes, after we're dead?

Woman: I suppose that's true. But there is something I wonder.

Director: Oh?

Woman: I think there are two types of full justice.

Director: What two?

Woman: The kind that deals with the surface, and the kind that deals with the heart.

SURFACE

Director: I imagine both are hard to deliver.

Woman: But surely you think the surface justice is the easier of the two.

Director: I don't know. The heart is certainly hard to know; but so are all the facts. And, now that we mention it, I suppose there is no way to judge the heart *except* through the facts.

Woman: Who said anything about judging?

Director: What do you think full justice is?

Woman: Full justice is the full picture, not some judgment yea or nay.

Director: Each brush stroke in the articulation of justice *is* a yea or nay. And let's remember—the finest painting in the world is nothing but surface with the *appearance* of depth.

Woman: So what are you saying? The heart doesn't really exist?

Director: Of course not. But unless we choose to share it ourselves, no one has full access to it.

Woman: And even then we might lie.

Director: Sure. So we have to rely on the surface and infer the state of the heart.

Woman: I suppose that's true. And I think there are two types of people here. One, those who feel most comfortable when they can share the state of their heart. Two, those who feel most comfortable when they lock their heart away.

Director: You surprise me. I would have thought you'd say no one can be comfortable when they lock their heart away. What kind of person is?

Woman: Someone who's suffered trauma.

Director: So only the damaged lock their heart away?

Woman: Who else would?

Director: Someone who's looking for freedom.

Woman: You can't be serious.

Director: What is freedom?

Woman: The opposite of tyranny.

Director: Well, if someone or something is trying to tyrannize over our heart....

Woman: We should resist.

Director: It's best to resist when your heart is secure. Do you agree?

Woman: I agree.

Director: Can we be secure when we let a tyrant into our depths?

Woman: Of course not. But we let those we love come in.

Director: And that's why when attempting full justice we need to interview loved ones and friends.

Woman: Loved ones and friends. Friends are loved ones, you know.

Director: Not always.

Woman: But if they're not, why would we let them into our heart?

Director: Sometimes we make mistakes.

Woman: We think we love them but we don't? How is that possible? If you love, you love.

Director: Let's look at it this way. Are your loved ones always friends?

Woman: Well, no.

Director: Why not?

Woman: Sometimes we're at odds.

Director: And yet we love them just the same?

Woman: Yes.

Director: Why?

Woman: Let's get clear what we're talking about. By 'loved ones' people usually mean family.

Director: And by friends they mean loved ones who aren't family, strictly speaking.

Woman: But some friends *are* family.

Director: And some friends aren't.

GRIEF

Woman: We take comfort in loved ones and friends.

Director: When they really are loved and really are friends. How about your friend in surgery now?

Woman: She is *loved*. And your friend?

Director: The same. When do we take comfort in them?

Woman: What do you mean?

Director: Are you taking comfort in her right now?

Woman: I... don't know. Can we be comfortable when drowned in worry?

Director: I suppose we might be, if we know the comfort will be there when we dry ourselves off.

Woman: But what if... she dies? The comfort won't be there no matter how dry I am.

Director: A part of us and memories.

Woman: What are you talking about?

Director: Do you agree our friends become a part of us?

Woman: I certainly do.

Director: And do you believe memories can comfort?

Woman: Yes.

Director: Then a part of the comfort will be there once the worry stops and we remember our friend.

Woman: But that part is much smaller than our grief.

Director: That's up to us.

Woman: No, no way. You can't tell me we can control our grief. Grief is a force of nature, a terrible thing.

Director: I was thinking of 'that part', not the grief. We nurture that of them that's in us; we keep the memories strong.

Woman: And if grief is stronger nonetheless?

Director: Would you believe me if I tell you some people find comfort in their grief?

Woman: Does that make grief a good thing?

Director: I don't know. Is comfort always good?

Woman: No, and I do know people who take comfort in grief. They never move on.

Director: They're used to grief and make it their bed.

Woman: What can be done?

Director: Nothing. They have to do it on their own.

Woman: But people like this strike me as being incapable of that.

Director: Let's be sure we're talking about the same thing. If someone we love dies, we'll always feel some degree of loss, of grief. But some of us let this grief, long after the loss, dominate their lives.

Woman: Yes, that's what I'm talking about. Unhealthy grief.

Director: Grief as a crutch?

Woman: Grief as a crutch.

Director: And we take comfort in our crutch.

Woman: This comfort is bad.

Director: Why?

Woman: Think of it like lying in bed all day instead of going out for a run.

Director: So comfort isn't always good.

Woman: It's not. It can lead to decay.

Conversations 2

Director: Decay. Decadence. A falling away.

Woman: A falling away from health.

Director: We need to make ourselves uncomfortable at times.

Woman: I completely agree. When does that happen for you?

Director: When I have conversations.

Woman: I thought you love to have conversations.

Director: I do; but there are conversations within conversations—and some of them are uncomfortable indeed.

Woman: What do you mean? Conversations within conversations.

Director: The obvious case is when a conversation lends itself to different levels of meaning. What I'm thinking of now is when we have monologues within, during the dialogue without.

Woman: So there are, barring different levels of meaning, three conversations at once—a dialogue and two monologues.

Director: In an active conversation, yes.

Woman: What's an inactive conversation?

Director: Anything less than that.

Woman: And that's the falling away? That lack of multiple voices?

Director: Yes. And I'm glad you brought up voices. Harmony with all three is a comfort to hear. Dissonance is uncomfortable at best.

Woman: And if you're not musical?

Director: If you don't care if something is harmonious or not? Is that what you're asking?

Woman: Yes, there are people like that, you know.

Director: I do. I've even heard that there are musicians like this.

Woman: It's true. They don't *feel* the music. It's a purely technical exercise on their part. I suppose there are philosophers like this.

Director: Oh, yes—without a doubt.

Woman: I think they have an advantage. Where dissonance might bring a musical philosopher to a halt, they plow right through.

Director: True. Does that make them healthy or decadent?

Woman: Who says decadents can't be healthy?

Director: Can you explain?

Woman: Both types of philosophers can, in my thinking, be healthy. Decadents aren't brought low by a little musical friction. But musical philosophers are sensitive to things the others can't discern.

Director: What if they know how to keep the dialogue healthy but let their own internal monologue scream in atonal noise?

Woman: I'd feel sorry for them.

Director: But it's all sound and fury signifying nothing. It has no negative effect.

Woman: Lack of beauty *is* a negative effect.

Director: So three-way beauty is best—dialogue and dual monologues.

Woman: Yes,

Director: But how would we ever know? At best we hear two-way beauty—that of the dialogue and our own.

Woman: There must be a way to infer from the dialogue the other person's inner state.

Director: We'd have to set traps.

Woman: Yes, I like that. But how?

Director: We throw in dissonant concepts now and then and see if it bothers them.

Woman: Yes, but remember—they are technical masters. They know what goes with what. They'll call us on the concept-tone, even though it doesn't bother them in the least.

Director: Then we need to break new ground.

Woman: They won't know what goes where! They'll have to feel their way through! Yes, that's the only way to flush them out of the bush.

Director: How do we know what goes where?

Woman: We *feel* it, Director. We simply feel it.

UNCOMFORTABLE

Director: Are you saying if we feel uncomfortable we know they're false?

Woman: And if comfortable we know they're true.

Director: But what if we're uncomfortable with the truth?

Woman: Well....

Director: The dialogue, we can tell if it's true—yes, if we search with all our might. Our monologue, we can test and prove it true or false—so long as we're honest with ourselves. But the monologue of the other? I don't think we have access to that.

Woman: We're all islands in the stream?

Director: Maybe only some of us are. But people like us? Yes. Islands in the stream.

Woman: I'm not sure I'm comfortable with that.

Director: Maybe I should say we *live on* islands in the stream. And we take our boats and visit each other now and then.

Woman: I like that much better. I like the idea of having my own island. But I do want company, now and then. Life would be so much better if we could regulate whom we have for company when. What do we do if boats just keep showing up uninvited on our shore?

Director: We make it uncomfortable for them.

Woman: How?

Director: We play the dissonant to their tune.

Woman: And if they don't care?

Director: Dissonance is, by definition, what people don't like. I think we can drive them away.

Woman: And if we can't?

Director: Then we have to wonder why they're there.

Woman: Some people are obtuse. They can't take a hint. We have to tell them in no uncertain terms that they must go.

Director: And if they have some claim on us?

Woman: Then we're in for quite an uncomfortable time. But what claim could they have?

Director: Oh, I don't know. Some lie we told in the past? Rather than confront them with the difficult truth, we told them an easy lie. That's their claim. They believed and acted on the untruth. And now we don't like to admit what we did.

Woman: What's the gist of the lie?

Director: That we are good friends. That we like them for what they are.

Woman: But the truth is that they make us uncomfortable. They don't allow us to be what we are. Some people just chatter about senseless things. I don't chatter back. That's not who I am. So I remain silent and nod and smile. And that's a sort of terrible lie.

Director: Oh, don't be so hard on yourself. But I do have one suggestion. Drop the nod and keep the smile.

Woman: The smile of contempt?

Director: That's one interpretation.

Woman: You want me to be a sphinx.

Director: Sphinxes don't suffer the torment of conscience for their smiles.

Woman: I'll tell *you* the truth. I'm afraid I'll get a reputation—and it will impact my work.

Director: You're already first chair. What impact do you fear?

Woman: It's a long way to fall from the top.

Director: The art world loves an enigma.

Woman: At a remove. Not first hand.

Director: Well, I love an enigma.

Woman: But you want to figure it out.

Director: Of course. I want to make the enigmatic my friends.

Woman: Excuse me for asking, but what if they don't want to be friends with you?

Director: The sphinx *wants* to be unriddled. I'm good at that.

Woman: In ancient mythology the sphinx killed itself after it was unriddled.

Director: Those Greeks loved to exaggerate a bit.

FRIENDS 2

Woman: So are you saying you know how to make the uncomfortable comfortable?

Director: Yes. But I don't always act on my knowledge.

Woman: That's a terrible thing. Why wouldn't you?

Director: Some people deserve to be uncomfortable.

Woman: Yes, but they're not the people who are uncomfortable most of the time. They're the ones who make others uncomfortable most of the time.

Director: True. If I can make an innocent comfortable, I do.

Woman: Are sphinxes innocent?

Director: What do *you* think?

Woman: No.

Director: Why not? Aren't they merely protecting themselves? Don't they drop their guard with friends?

Woman: After a while I'm not sure it's merely protection.

Director: What could it be?

Woman: An ice cold pleasure.

Director: Ah. And you're afraid they come to prefer this pleasure to having friends?

Woman: Sphinxes are alone.

Director: Not if they can be unriddled.

Woman: How many sphinxes do you have as friends?

Director: None. But you should ask how many former sphinxes do I have as friends. And the answer is three.

Woman: You've unriddled *three*?

Director: I've unriddled many more than three. But three stuck around.

Woman: Why do you think they did?

Director: It was convenient.

Woman: That's it? Convenient?

Director: Would it be better if I said it's because they're comfortable here?

Woman: Yes, I think it would.

Director: Why?

Woman: Convenience is... base.

Director: Haven't you heard of creature comfort?

Woman: Yes, yes. But in comfort we're talking about something *moral* here.

Director: Moral? Because it has to do with friends? I think that's a mistake.

Woman: Why a mistake? What is moral and pure if not the love of friends?

Director: Morality, purity, love, friendship. You ask a lot in that little question of yours. What is friendship?

Woman: A love where you can be yourself.

Director: The being yourself is what's pure.

Woman: And the love.

Director: Okay. But why not stop there? Why add morality to the mix? Is it necessary?

Woman: It's.... I don't know. Why *wouldn't* it be necessary?

Director: You want me to prove a negative? Why aren't fish dogs?

Woman: Oh, stop. I take the point. So the question is why *would* it be necessary. I guess... it wouldn't.

Director: What made you think for a moment it might?

Woman: Morality protects.

Director: Against others who might otherwise do the friends in? It's a defense?

Woman: Yes, a defense. It lends a sort of legitimacy to things.

Director: And that's part of the trouble—to *things.* We're not talking about just any old thing. We're speaking of friends.

MORALITY

Woman: Yes, but I spoke to quickly. Morality doesn't legitimize anything. It only legitimizes certain types of things.

Director: What doesn't it legitimize?

Woman: And now you're the one with the negative! But I'll answer. It doesn't legitimize conversations like this.

Director: Why not? I think it's a perfectly good conversation. Are we promoting anything bad? Are we here under false pretenses? Are we harming one another?

Woman: No, no, and no.

Director: Are you uncomfortable with our conversation?

Woman: Are you? I *know* the answer is no. And it's no for me. I just get the feeling that there are people who would think this much comfort between two people is... wrong.

Director: Why would it be wrong?

Woman: Because it's exclusive—it excludes.

Director: I'd be happy to have another friend join us.

Woman: But I'm not thinking of friends. I'm thinking of... enemies.

Director: Yes, we shouldn't let the enemies in.

Woman: But seriously, sometimes jealous people, they... they....

Director: Burn witches at the stake.

Woman: Yes! Exactly! That's what they do!

Director: And 'witches' are immoral. Tell me, who are they who can confer 'morality' on another—legitimacy, or whatever?

Woman: The same inquisitors who burn.

Director: Do you think it's a stretch to say they burn because their victims make them uncomfortable?

Woman: No, no stretch at all.

Director: But they don't care if we're uncomfortable.

Woman: They couldn't care less.

Director: Is it a stretch to say morality, or 'morality', protects the comfort of the judges?

Woman: Again, no stretch at all. I think it can be defined as that which protects comfort.

Director: But we—you and I and our friends—don't employ such comfort saving devices, do we?

Woman: Well....

Director: If we don't, maybe we should?

Woman: It's a fair question to ask. Don't we deserve some protection?

Director: The protection we spoke of is a naked smile. Is that as bad as burning someone at the stake?

Woman: Of course not. And I don't care what they say. We're not immoral. There's nothing wrong with us. In fact, there's lots of good. Friendship is good. Love is good. Honesty is good. Courage is good.

Director: Yes, but now I'm wondering. Why do we have to protect those nouns with the adjective 'good'? Can't we just say 'friendship' and know what it is, and let it stand on its own? Do you know what I mean? Do you see what I'm trying to say?

Woman: I do know what you mean. 'Good' here is a sort of defense. And why should we be defensive? When I say 'honesty', all our true friends know what that means. And I think our enemies do, too.

Director: Yes, but they call it different things. It's not honesty, it's brazenness.

Woman: Yes, it's disrespect, and so on.

Director: They have a perverted notion of respect.

Woman: Yes, they call it 'respect' but it's really something else.

Director: What is it?

Woman: It's... it's.... I wish I knew.

TRUTH

Director: Maybe it's an agreed upon stifling of the truth?

Woman: Something like that, sure. The truth is not the truth. It's an agreed upon set of premises, a sort of contract. 'I won't say this about you; you won't say that about me.'

Director: And then along comes someone like you, who says this and that.

Woman: Right. And I think it works the other way, too. They agree not just *not* to say certain things. They agree to *say* certain things.

Director: To falsify the words.

Woman: Yes. They call dishonesty 'honesty'. They call cowardice 'courage'. Pretty much the opposites of all things.

Director: How do they get away with it?

Woman: I don't know. But the roots are ancient. Pilate asked, 'What is truth?' A lot of people refer to this as 'jesting Pilate'. But I never thought he was kidding. I think he meant the question sincerely. He asked because he lived in a world where truth stood on its head.

Director: Has the world ever not stood truth on its head?

Woman: Well, that's a problem. Because then how would we know what truth is? It's always the upside down person in the room? That's how I often feel—no, *always* feel in a crowded room.

Director: Is that why you turned to music? It's where you can be in a room, part of group, and they all speak truth?

Woman: I never thought about it that way before. I think you're right. 'Shut up and play the score!' That's what I want. I want the score; but I also want... silence from them.

Director: Is some music more honest?

Woman: Some music tells the truth. Some music lies.

Director: That's a sort of mystery to me. How can you tell?

Woman: I don't know. It's just a sense I have. Some music is *clean*.

Director: Clean in how it makes you feel?

Woman: Yes. Don't strike me with fear then suggest it's love. Does that make any sense?

Director: Can't we be afraid of love?

Woman: Well, yes—of course. I should give you a better example. Don't present sweet innocence then entangle it in decadent sophistication.

Director: You mean, don't present Eve and the snake?

Woman: I'm not doing a very good job. There *is* such a thing as emotional truth. It's just something you feel rather than know.

Director: I believe you. But let me ask you this. Assuming your own emotions are true, can't we say music is honest when you feel comfort in it?

Woman: Yes. Truth loves honesty and feels good in it.

Director: Why does truth love honesty? I mean, aren't there times when the truth doesn't want to be revealed?

Woman: You mean like our sphinx. I hadn't thought of that. But the sphinx wants to be unriddled. Otherwise, why pose the riddle at all?

Director: An excellent point. But maybe truth wants a witness who can understand what the truth *means*.

Woman: That's what a great composer wants—a listener who *knows*.

Director: Maybe that's what all of us want, even the bad.

Woman: The funny thing about knowing the bad is that there's not much to know. It's usually just some little rotten thing that defines their whole life. Do they want it known? Maybe. But something tells them how pathetic it is, and they resist, blowing themselves up like monsters of the deep—for something shallow in the end.

Director: But monsters of the deep in the shallows will drown.

Woman: Then we should never be deep with the bad.

Director: That's very good advice. But are the bad really that uncomfortable in the shallows?

Woman: They're comfortable being shallow for very many things. They are *uncomfortable* when it touches on their hidden sore. A lore grows up around the sore that makes them seem profound.

Director: A lore grows up? You mean they create their own lore.

Woman: They create their own 'truth'. And a rotten truth it is.

'TRUTH'

Director: 'Truth' becomes its own sort of truth.

Woman: But the truth is that every 'truth' is the same.

Director: Yes, that's true. How many people does that amount to as same?

Woman: Very many.

Director: The majority?

Woman: Yes. Why, don't you agree?

Director: It might even be a super-majority.

Woman: Ha, ha. Yes. But maybe we should qualify things. Almost everyone has a 'truth'. But not everyone has a fatal 'truth'.

Director: 'Almost everyone' and 'not everyone'? What's the difference?

Woman: Oh, you know what I mean. I'm just saying there are sins and then there are deadly sins.

Director: I don't know. I know the old saying, 'Who of us is without sin?' I know it implies we shouldn't *judge*. But I think we should *try*.

Woman: Try to get rid of untruth.

Director: Yes. Untruths, no matter how small, are deadly.

Woman: You really expect perfect truth? I think that's a dream. In fact, I think that expectation is somehow... false. I hope you know what I mean. I'm not trying to offend.

Director: 'Truth' is the spice of life—when in the right hands. How's that?

Woman: Ha, ha. Is it true? Do we need lies?

Director: Maybe we do.

Woman: But not lies to ourselves.

Director: Maybe especially to ourselves.

Woman: Give me an example of such a lie.

Director: We lie that we understand our friends.

Woman: When we don't. Well, I can see some truth in that. If we didn't tell that lie, we might lose them as our friends. But doesn't the lie prevent us from *trying* to understand?

Director: Our discomfort in the untruth will prompt us to try.

Woman: That's interesting. The untruth is a sort of spur. If we use the lie judiciously, we might urge ourselves to grow. But then I have two questions. Why do some people not feel discomfort with the lie? And why do some who do fail to grow?

Director: Maybe this is a lie I tell myself, but I think there are different kinds of people in the world. The untruth or truth affects us differently.

Woman: We're not all the same. Which means we're not all equal. I'm on board with that. It's just odd that discomfort and growth bring out this fact, if we can call it a fact. But really, is it fiction?

Director: Let's be scientific about it and call it a working hypothesis.

Woman: Well, the data I've seen in my life tells me it's true. How about you?

Director: The data I've seen tells me that if it isn't true, it might be necessary.

Woman: Necessary for whom?

Director: For us, our friends.

Woman: Why?

Director: I gives us space.

Woman: There aren't enough islands to go round?

Director: Something like that.

Woman: I'd be willing to lie for you.

Director: And I would lie for you.

Woman: But I think I would also be willing to lie *to you.*

Director: And I would never lie to you.

Woman: You just did!

Director: Ha! You caught me in a lie?

Woman: If you have to ask....

Director: Tell me what lie.

Woman: You've been suggesting all along that you care about comfort.

Director: I do.

Woman: But you don't care about it *most.*

Director: I thought that's what I said. But even if I didn't—what's wrong with that?

Woman: That question, coming from you, is a lie.

IRONY

Director: There's a difference between irony and lies.

Woman: Tell me what irony is.

Director: Socratic playing dumb.

Woman: You don't think playing dumb is a lie?

Director: Not when it's in self- or other-defense.

Woman: What's other-defense?

Director: Protecting someone by pretending not to know. Surely you've done that before. No?

Woman: Well, I have. And you know I'm not upset with your irony on me.

Director: But now that I've spoken of other-defense, I'm not sure it's good.

Woman: Didn't we say we'd avoid the adjective 'good'?

Director: I don't know what other-defense is.

Woman: That's better. But you just said! And I'll add to your definition. Other-defense is a lie told to protect someone you know.

Director: But there's nothing ironic about that. Irony here is the key. I'll concede that other-defense is a lie—but it's an ironic lie.

Woman: Now you know what other-defense is! And I don't care if it's good. I would employ it any day.

Director: Because you protect your friends. So do I. But the bad also protect their friends.

Woman: They do so in order to protect themselves. When we protect, we're taking a risk.

Director: What's the risk?

Woman: That the lie will wreck the friendship. And not because the other finds out. The lie might cause us discomfort. This might cause us to act differently than we otherwise would. This difference might create friction in the friendship. And that might mean the end.

Director: I know what you mean. I also think lie begets lie, so it only makes worse what you describe. But let me ask you in earnest. What's wrong with a world of gentle, well-meaning lies?

Woman: Sometimes lies are sweet. But we can't live on sugar and spice.

Director: Well said. Truth is like meat.

Woman: I'd rather say it's like protein. I don't eat any meat.

Director: Then protein it is. Why don't you eat meat?

Woman: It's not on principle, or for health, or whatever. I just like animals too much. But let's not dwell on this. I'm not trying to convert anyone or justify myself. I'm just not comfortable with meat. Did you ever go hunting?

Director: I've been hunting, yes.

Woman: Did you kill?

Director: I did.

Woman: Did you eat what you killed?

Director: Yes.

Woman: You see, I can stomach that for you—just not for me.

Director: There are different kinds of truth.

Woman: Yes. Thanks for getting us back to the point. We have to find the truth that suits our stomach well.

Director: I'm having a hard time thinking of where to take the metaphor next. Do we say friends are those whose tastes are the same? Do our enemies never eat protein? Do *we* eat nothing *but* protein? If not, what sort of lies flavor 'meat' best?

Woman: Yes, we may be painting ourselves into a corner here. But really— who paints the floor?

Opposites

Director: Metaphors shape our lives.

Woman: Yes, that's something I understand. Certain metaphors comfort; others frighten. Either way they shape our lives.

Director: Have we hit upon something new? A new opposite? We've spoken of comfort and its opposite discomfort. But fear is an opposite, too. No?

Woman: We seek comfort when we fear, yes. But you know we, some of us, seek courage when we fear. And courage is a better opposite than comfort. Don't you agree?

Director: We're both here fearing for our friend. Is our conversation one of courage or comfort?

Woman: I'd say it's a little of both. There's nothing wrong with that. In fact, courage and comfort *should* go together. They belong together. They strengthen one another.

Director: You have a good—I mean, you have a point. A forceful point. I'd like courageous comfort and comfortable courage. Who wouldn't? It takes armchair quarterbacking to a new level.

Woman: You can just tell me I'm wrong, you know.

Director: Seriously, I think you're right. But now I'm wondering if there are any more opposites we should explore. Discomfort. Fear. What else?

Woman: Confusion.

Director: Confusion? I don't understand. In fact, I'm confused. What's the typically understood opposite of confusion?

Woman: Clarity.

Director: Ah, clarity—yes. But I'm not so sure it's opposite is the opposite of comfort, too. When we're confused, aren't we afraid? And we've already spoken of fear.

Woman: Not everyone is afraid when confused.

Director: What are they?

Woman: Confused. There's no other word. Confusion is a sort of discomfort, but it's sort of not. Do you think we can be comfortable while confused?

Director: You make me think of the phrase dazed and confused. But, no. To me confusion is an uncomfortable state. But it's not simply discomfort. I'll allow it as an opposite. Discomfort. Fear. Confusion. What else?

Woman: I can't think of anything else. Can you? If yes, I'll see if I can find it in me to *allow* it in.

Director: Touché. I can't think of anything else. But while we're on the topic of opposites, can metaphors have an opposite?

Woman: I don't see why not. Let's have an example.

Director: Alright. Comfort is a happy stomach. The opposite of a happy stomach—

Woman: —is something we don't need to discuss. Well, we have our opposite. Should we go around reversing enemy metaphors?

Director: I think that's an excellent habit to be in. But, to be sure, they'll turn ours around, too. They'll turn them upside down. Is that a game we can win?

Woman: Aren't we more clever? Sure we can win! We just need—to run away when we're done.

Director: Live to fight another day? I'm fine with that. But, eventually, I think we have to make a stand.

Woman: How will we know when it's time?

Director: We'll no longer be able to run.

COWARDLY

Woman: That sounds a little cowardly, if you ask me.

Director: No one's stopping *you* from making a stand. Be as brave as you like. But when you sound the retreat, I'll be there to reinforce you as you fall back.

Woman: You'd reinforce a retreat? Does that make military sense?

Director: In the sense of friendship it sometimes does.

Woman: Why not reinforce the attack?

Director: Attacks like this are best made alone. They have more focus that way.

Woman: The enemy is strange. Some of their attacks are indiscriminate, others are as focused as can be. They have a knack for finding the single chink in the armor. Do you know what I mean?

Director: I do. But who says we need to wear armor? And if we must, let it be leather rather than chain or plate.

Woman: What's wrong with chain or plate?

Director: It's not very—comfortable. I like to be in comfort when I fight. In fact, that's often when I feel best.

Woman: Comfort and feeling our best aren't the same thing. Think of it this way. Let's say I win the Medal of Freedom for my work with the violin. As I go to receive the award my shoes are pinching my feet. I'm in great discomfort. And yet this is supposed to be the pinnacle of my life.

Director: Oh, you don't believe that award is any pinnacle, much less the ceremony you receive it in. Think of a better example.

Woman: In my *defense*, I did say it's *supposed* to be the pinnacle of my life.

Director: Don't play lawyer tricks on me. Let's ask the question. Can we be in discomfort and still feel our best? When do you feel your best?

Woman: When I finally master a difficult piece.

Director: Do you care if your shoes are pinching then?

Woman: I don't. I can't even feel my feet.

Director: Well, that's a different problem. But we share the point. Yes, it's nice if we don't feel discomfort. But at the critical moment—

Woman: —discomfort fades away. At once. And if it doesn't, the moment isn't what we think.

Director: The moment isn't what we think. I like that. What is it?

Woman: Something that's *supposed* to be the pinnacle, the highest we can reach. But we can reach higher. And the proof is in what we don't feel.

Director: A coward would tell himself that that moment *is* the moment. That he has reached as high as he can reach. He swallows the lie. It allows him not to make the effort to reach as far as he can.

Woman: And the lie gives him indigestion. No one can stomach a lie like this, though people tell them all the time.

Director: What's the result of the indigestion?

Woman: He feels sick all the time. And if sick, unable to reach his true height. So he needs to vomit the lie right up—and try again.

Director: And if he's afraid to try?

Woman: The lie will be his excuse to make no effort—to hide.

Director: I've often wondered why people hide.

Woman: It's because they're afraid. Afraid to be exposed.

Director: But our example is strange. Here we have someone who could do so much more. Why worry about being exposed for that? Isn't that a sort of compliment?

Woman: He doesn't believe in himself. What can you say?

Director: And that's a shameful thing? Not believing in yourself?

Woman: I think it is. You have to understand the motivation of the coward. Belief in yourself requires you to take steps, difficult steps—steps that lead you upward.

Director: The coward doesn't want to go up?

Woman: No, he very much wants to go up. But he's afraid of the steps. And maybe he's afraid of heights.

Director: What is it about the steps?

Woman: Like I said, they're difficult. They take effort, serious effort. And here's the secret about all cowards. They are, fundamentally—lazy.

LAZINESS

Director: Laziness and comfort are related, in some way at least.

Woman: What's nicer than spending a lazy day at home?

Director: Not spending ten lazy days at home—unless you don't mind the feeling of decay.

Woman: Laziness is only comfortable, for us, when we're resting from strenuous effort. Once rested, we need to return. We need to *earn* our laziness. Unearned laziness leads to—and is a symptom of—rot.

Director: Do you believe we can be comfortable in a spiritual way when making strenuous effort?

Woman: Absolutely. Whistle while you work.

Director: But 'work' isn't necessarily strenuous. I'm talking about something that's a real strain. Comfortable?

Woman: No, not if you're really pushing it hard. But, as they say, no pain no gain.

Director: Do we relax in greater comfort after we make the gain?

Woman: The gain happens *while* we relax, while we *recuperate.*

Director: I like that word. It comes from Latin for 'take back'. So while we're relaxing in comfort we're actually working to take back what's ours.

Woman: But the lazy never recuperate. They don't have it in them.

Director: Yes, but now I wonder. Suppose someone is very sick, and it's a great effort simply to go out and get the mail. They have to recover for an hour. Recuperation?

Woman: Well, sickness changes the story. The sick aren't lazy—they're... sick!

Director: Can we say laziness is a sickness?

Woman: That's turning things on their head. And it doesn't do justice to the sick!

Director: Could there be a danger we're failing to do justice to the lazy?

Woman: Well, we're not going to say if laziness is good or bad. We're just going to describe it for what it is. It's an unwillingness to act in a strenuous way. How's that?

Director: Pretty good. I guess that says it all. And sometimes we're comfortable in our laziness and sometimes we're not. When would we be not?

Woman: When we know there's something we need to do, something strenuous, that we cannot bring ourselves to do. I'd say we're uncomfortable then.

Director: Laziness has an ally, I think. Its name is inertia.

Woman: Yes, they're fast friends. The more lazy you are, the greater your friend.

Director: And the greater your friend, the greater the laziness, I'd venture. They complement one another well.

Woman: They create a self-sustaining ecosystem of their own. A swamp.

Director: Certain creatures love the swamp—alligators, for one. Are they lazy?

Woman: Maybe? I don't know. Don't they have to hunt all the time?

Director: Have you seen how they hunt?

Woman: They mostly lie in wait, don't they?

Director: I think so. I'll have to watch some late night animal t.v. to be sure. But what of any creature who mostly lies in wait? Spiders, for instance. What do we think of them? Lazy?

Woman: I have seen some amazing webs in my time. And when the web is rent, the spider simply sets to it again. Then they go back and wait.

Director: Is watching and waiting doing nothing?

Woman: I suppose it's not. It's watching and waiting. But I'm not giving any credit to those who are watching and waiting for the end of the world.

Director: You and I are watching and waiting right now.

Woman: True. I wish we had some news. Talking with you helps. The lazy can't talk like this. They can't keep *clean*.

Director: A clean conversation takes some doing. I have a friend who's an author. He wrote more than a hundred drafts of his book of conversation in order to make it clean. When you open a book it's like walking into a house. You know right away if it's clean.

Woman: But the kids' bedroom might be a mess.

Director: Yes, messy—but clean. There's a difference.

Woman: Your friend the author, you've been to his house?

Director: I have. It was neat, but not very clean.

Woman: What does that say about him?

Director: He strives in his work and exhausts his strength. Then? There's nothing but rest.

STRUGGLE

Woman: Do you strive in your work?

Director: I do my job, but I wouldn't say I strive.

Woman: How about in philosophy?

Director: I struggle to know things at times, but it's not really striving.

Woman: What's the difference between struggling and striving? Comfort?

Director: Can you say more?

Woman: Striving can be pleasant effort; struggling can't.

Director: We usually strive from ambition. Ambition is a worm that gnaws at the soul. Or I have I got it wrong?

Woman: Satisfied ambition makes us feel great. Satisfied struggle, so to speak, makes us feel relief—comfort.

Director: What if we don't take up the struggle? What if we don't engage?

Woman: Then we decay.

Director: Do you think there is comfort in decay?

Woman: Maybe initially. But eventually it makes us feel rotten.

Director: Is it possible at any point in our decline to take up the struggle?

Woman: It gets harder and harder the further we fall.

Director: Why?

Woman: Our struggle muscles atrophy.

Director: And there's more to struggle against?

Woman: Exactly.

Director: But we can take comfort in small victories.

Woman: We certainly can. It's hard to struggle once you've let go. But it's not impossible.

Director: What if we strive instead of struggling?

Woman: Our ambition is to get out of our mess?

Director: Why not?

Woman: I don't think that's the right use of 'ambition'.

Director: Can't we use it however we like?

Woman: We can. But at a certain point we stretch the truth too far.

Director: The truth is language based? The truth is all about words?

Woman: What isn't all about words?

Director: A look in the eye. A smile on the face.

Woman: Yes, that's true. I don't know. I suppose we can say it's our ambition to stop the decay.

Director: What's the opposite of decay?

Woman: Growth.

Director: We can certainly have an ambition to grow.

Woman: And we certainly can struggle to grow.

Director: Why would we?

Woman: Because we want to—and growth is hard. Tell me. Why do you prefer struggle to striving?

Director: Because ambition is uncomfortable.

Woman: Why? I suppose if it's an intense ambition it could be. But what about a mild ambition?

Director: A mild ambition isn't an ambition. It's a sort of dream. Ambition is all consuming. There's nothing comfortable about that.

MONSTROUS

Woman: I know ambitious people who aren't all consumed.

Director: They're either lying or aren't that ambitious.

Woman: Why would they lie? What would that prove?

Director: It would prove they aren't monsters. Anything taken too far is monstrous.

Woman: Even comfort?

Director: Sure, even comfort.

Woman: How about love? Is it monstrous to love too dearly?

Director: Love is the greatest monster.

Woman: Now you're just teasing. But tell me why that's so.

Director: Do you agree that ambition can be monstrous?

Woman: Of course.

Director: Do you agree that love can trump ambition?

Woman: Definitely.

Director: Well, there you have it. Love is more monstrous than ambition.

Woman: Oh, that's a rotten argument! Is it even an argument? I'm not sure. I think it's just something you said.

Director: I was struggling to tell the truth. Maybe one day I'll succeed.

Woman: Not like that, you won't. What does it mean to be monstrous?

Director: To be ugly or frightening.

Woman: That's a strange definition. Ugly and frightening are two very different things.

Director: You think ugliness isn't frightening?

Woman: Ugliness is just ugliness. I don't know why anyone would be afraid.

Director: Okay. But is frightfulness ugly?

Woman: I don't know. I can imagine a beauty so intense that it's frightening. Can't you?

Director: I don't know. I think we're running into trouble with definitions again. You don't want to play word games, do you?

Woman: No I don't. That's what I didn't like about philosophy in college. It seemed to be a big game, a sort of inside joke. It was distasteful.

Director: Do game playing philosophers have any ambition?

Woman: I don't see how they could. And if they did, it would simply be to seem very clever.

Director: What would an ambitious philosopher look like? What would they do?

Woman: I think they would try to rule the world with thought.

Director: Which means to rule it with words.

Woman: Yes, it does. We all know the world can't be ruled with words.

Director: Don't be so sure. We think in words. If someone controls the words we use to think, isn't that a sort of control over us?

Woman: Then Webster of the Dictionary is the greatest philosophical ruler ever! Look at you smile!

Director: You make an excellent point. I love to smile at excellent points. Webster may have been a man of terrible ambition. A monster of language.

Woman: Are poets monsters of language?

Director: Ah, poets. Poets are lovers of words, some of them monstrous— yes. They want to milk every word for all its meaning, bleed them dry onto the page.

Woman: Milk and blood. You have something of the poet in you, Director. And it—amuses me!

Director: Ha! Well, I'm glad to amuse a lovely like you. But I don't like to amuse my enemies—unless I'm setting a trap.

Woman: Are your enemies the monsters of ambition?

Director: Some of them are.

Woman: And some of your friends are, too.

AMBITION

Director: Some ambition serves a great purpose. But it has to be used in the proper way upon the proper things.

Woman: Now you know you have to tell me two things. What's the proper way; what are the proper things?

Director: The proper way is *senza rispetto.*

Woman: Without respect? For what?

Director: Anything.

Woman: Complete ruthlessness?

Director: Absolute ruthlessness.

Woman: And what are the proper things?

Director: Those who deserve no ruth.

Woman: Well, there's your trick. Who deserves no respect? I suppose you'll say it's the rotten, the decayed, those who never try, those who never struggle.

Director: You guessed very well. But never try? Try at what?

Woman: To know.

Director: Know what?

Woman: Themselves.

Director: Oh, that's not it. People live very full lives every day without a shred of self-knowledge. The trial is with something else.

Woman: The trial? Try, trial. I like that. What else could it be? Maybe they never try to know the world.

Director: Hmm. I think there's some truth in that. But there are different sorts of world to know.

Woman: What sorts are there?

Director: Think of terrain. There are flatlands. There are mountains. There is ocean There is desert. If you live in one of those places, that's your world. So there are different worlds to know.

Woman: What's our world like?

Director: That's one of my ambitions. I'd like to know what our world is like.

Woman: Not just *your* world, where you live? But all of the world? Then again, you did say *our* world. Who is *we*?

Director: You're a regular bag of questions. I like that about you.

Woman: I hope I'm not an *old* bag of questions.

Director: You are certainly not. You're also not a bag of old questions. There's something fresh in your questions today.

Woman: The only thing fresh about them is that they are diverting us from worrying about our friends.

Director: They are doing that. But they're doing something more. They're making me think. What is our world like? That's my ambition. That's what I want to know.

Woman: And my ambition is to know who is *we*.

Director: *We* right now is you and me. What's our world like?

Woman: Our world is like an apple—and we will take a bite! What do you think of that?

Director: This raises an interesting problem. I asked what the world is *like* and you responded with a metaphor. That's very appropriate. So I have to ask what the world *is*.

Woman: That's harder to answer. Right now the world is this waiting room, Director.

Director: Yes, that's a good start. What can we say about this room?

Woman: It's not very comfortable. And that's odd because you would think of all the rooms that need comfort, this one is it.

Director: Why do you think they chose to make this room uncomfortable?

Woman: Well, I wouldn't say they *chose* to make it uncomfortable. They probably didn't have enough money.

Director: They chose to put the money to other use.

Woman: True enough.

Director: What makes it uncomfortable?

Woman: It's barren, and the chairs are hard. That'll do it. By the way, you don't know how glad I am you turned off the television. That *distraction* is not a distraction to me. Or rather, it distracts me from my thoughts. And I don't want that. I like our conversation because it *stirs* my thoughts. And I have a suspicion.

Director: Oh?

Woman: I suspect stirring thought is your *greatest* ambition.

UNRIDDLED

Director: Well, you've gone and figured me out. What can I say? Maybe I'm a monster here?

Woman: There are worse monsters in the world, and you know it. I don't think stirring thought is so bad.

Director: Maybe you haven't had the right thought stirred. People do resist thinking, you know. So it's something of a struggle.

Woman: *Something* of a struggle? I'd say it's an out-and-out struggle, if anything is. People resist thought as though it were the most terrible thing in the world. But what's the *right* thought for me?

Director: I don't know. We haven't hit upon it yet.

Woman: How can you tell? Maybe I've already had my thought and you're in the dark.

Director: It wouldn't be the first time I've been in the dark. Still, I think I could tell. If you had your thought a long time ago, I'd sense a certain inner comfort in you. If you've yet to have it, I'd sense a certain tension.

Woman: What do you sense, O wise one?

Director: I should hasten to add—there can be more than one thought. I sense comfort *and* tension in you.

Woman: So I've thought some and have more to think. Not surprising. I sense the same in you. And I sense this. You stir thought *in order* to discover the world.

Director: Can't I stir thought simply because I like to stir thought?

Woman: I don't think you do anything *just because*. I sense purpose in you.

Director: I do want to know the world. But maybe I misspoke when I said it was my ambition. I'm not really sure I have any ambition at all.

Woman: Do you distinguish purpose from ambition?

Director: Yes, much the way we distinguished struggle from striving.

Woman: Purpose is good; ambition is bad?

Director: It's not that simple. But I have more purpose than ambition, I think it's fair to say.

Woman: Who cares if it's fair? I want to know if it's true.

Director: I think it's true. And maybe this is what it is. My purpose is to stir thought in order that we all might know the world.

Woman: Again, who is *we*?

Director: You, me, and our friends.

Woman: Oh, our friends. Do you think we could have this conversation if they were here?

Director: We wouldn't have *this* conversation. But we would have a conversation. No two conversations are alike—even and especially when about the same things.

Woman: If you had to sum up what our conversation is about, what would it be?

Director: Comfort. That's what we keep coming back to. Do you agree?

Woman: I'm not sure we can say it all in one word. I don't think I could summarize it for my friend. What did we talk about? Many things.

Director: Yes, but those many things centered on a theme.

Woman: Maybe. And maybe that was just accident.

Director: There are good accidents and bad accidents.

Woman: Well, ours—if we had one—was good.

Director: Why do you resist the idea of an accident?

Woman: Because we are both steering the conversation a certain way.

Director: Steering it toward comfort? Do you think that's what I'm doing?

Woman: We are two people in need of comfort at the moment. Are you doing it? Am I? Yes, but maybe not consciously. We all steer toward the things we need when we need them.

Director: I take your point but I think you're wrong on one thing. We don't *all* steer toward what we need. Some aren't such good pilots that way.

ASCETICS

Woman: Do you think they do this on purpose?

Director: I do—as a matter of will. They will themselves away from what they need.

Woman: Why would they do that? Do you think they do it as a matter of principle?

Director: I do, exactly that. There are ascetics who oppose comfort on principle. Have you ever met one?

Woman: I think that type is rare. There aren't very many ascetics left in the world. They belong to another age.

Director: Maybe this is a truth about our world we need to know.

Woman: Maybe? Do *you* see lots of ascetics running around?

Director: I don't.

Woman: Why do you sound sad?

Director: Do I? Philosophy once had to fight ascetics. But now it almost wishes they were back.

Woman: Why would philosophy wish that? And by *philosophy* do you simply mean you?

Director: You're right to ask. I am a philosopher. I identify myself with philosophy. But I am not philosophy whole.

Woman: Well, that's a relief! What can one *say* to philosophy whole? So why nostalgia for ascetics?

Director: They make such good enemies.

Woman: You mean they're tough?

Director: No, I mean it's a real pleasure to see when they lose. Their defeat brings them pleasure, which eventually brings them comfort.

Woman: Pleasure is how they lose? But who takes comfort in loss?

Director: I wish he had an ascetic here to ask. You have to be very gentle with them. Not all of them, of course. Some of them deserve being hit with a stick. But others are very gentle, very considerate. These are the ones to fight.

Woman: What sense does that make? You fight the ones you like? What's wrong with being gentle and considerate?

Director: Nothing. But they need to turn that gentleness and consideration toward themselves. They have to be part of their all, if that makes sense.

Woman: That does make sense. You are the bringer of comfort to ascetics. A noble thing. But how do you win?

Director: I have to find the desire for comfort within them. And then I speak sweet reason.

Woman: You don't argue with them?

Director: Argue? Not in the sense of a harangue, if that's what you mean. I speak more gently with them than anyone else—because they're quick to retreat into their shell.

Woman: Their shell of discomfort. Why choose discomfort on principle? It just seems so wrong.

Director: It's a sort of self-punishment for bad desires.

Woman: Do you think there are bad desires?

Director: I know there are imprudent desires. That's what we usually mean by bad.

Woman: I've never heard that before. How can that be what I mean by bad?

Director: We can mean things we don't know. It happens all the time.

Woman: Are we more comfortable when we know?

Director: Not always, no. In fact, I'd say we're often more comfortable when we don't know—at least at the time.

Woman: What does that mean?

Director: Maybe I'm only speaking a comforting belief. But it seems to me there are consequences when we don't know, unpleasant consequences. Ignorance protects us in the moment; it makes us pay later on.

Woman: Oh, I don't believe that for a moment. The ignorant stay ignorant and in this they find bliss.

Director: Would you take their bliss away?

Woman: I'd render them ascetic if I could.

PUNISHMENT

Director: Asceticism as other inflicted punishment. A novel idea. How would it work? You'd reason with them and persuade them discomfort is best?

Woman: Now I'm not so sure. Maybe ascetics are comfortable in their abstentions? Maybe the indulgences they deny actually make them uncomfortable?

Director: Yes, a good psychological insight. So to make someone an ascetic we have to make indulgence uncomfortable for them.

Woman: There's only one way to do that. Bad experience. We make their experience of pleasures bad. Retreat into asceticism then seems good.

Director: And it's as simple as that. Well, ignorant beware! But you'll have to tell us how you'll make pleasures bad.

Woman: Who can say how? But when there's a will, there's a way.

Director: A will to punish ignorance. Whence the will?

Woman: Ignorance does unknowing harm.

Director: So it's innocent?

Woman: In a sense. But it needs to know. I want to make it know.

Director: You almost sound like a philosopher.

Woman: Why only almost? Who knows? Maybe I'm a philosopher, too.

Director: And maybe you are. People typically think philosophy is all about knowing. By this they mean the philosopher wants to know. But philosophy might be all about making others know. Where I doubt is in whether this is punishment or not.

Woman: Knowing you've been an oaf is punishment, yes.

Director: Self-knowledge as punishment. Isn't that the idea behind penance and penitentiaries?

Woman: It is. But there is also joy in self-knowledge for those worth knowing.

Director: Ah, I like that. I'll seek to know myself in hopes of joy. What makes someone worth knowing?

Woman: Cleanliness.

Director: In thought? Yes, there's something to this. What about in the heart?

Woman: A clean heart? Yes, that's very appealing to me. A dirty heart is a tragedy.

Director: Is it punishment for your dirty heart to be known by another?

Woman: It is—a terrible punishment. People would kill the witness of this. If you're not your heart, what are you? And if your heart is dirty....

Director: Yes, terrible to be known. But really, who would want to know something like that? Would such knowledge be a burden? Who would carry it around?

Woman: The vengeful would welcome knowledge like this. They would take a profound comfort in their knowledge of the fact of the dirty heart.

Director: Is vengeance a bad desire? An imprudent desire? Something good to want?

Woman: It's not good to *want* vengeance; it's good to *have* vengeance. We take comfort in the having.

Director: Comfort or satisfaction?

Woman: Does it matter? No, I don't think it does. You don't need a word to know what you feel.

Director: And what you'd feel is good. But how do you know it's good? Is it just because you like the feeling? You enjoy the feeling?

Woman: I just want a feeling to enjoy, sure. And I don't care about communicating that feeling via words. It's mine alone.

Director: Darkness in feeling. But you really wouldn't try to share with a friend? You'd keep it all to yourself?

Woman: It's something you'd like to know, isn't it? Maybe if we trade....

Director: You'd want me to somehow share my most precious, wordless feeling? What happens when I give it words? Is it like the camera stealing my soul?

Woman: Maybe it is. Maybe we're doomed to enjoy—or to suffer—our feelings alone. Reward and punishment happen within, in the mechanism of the soul.

SOUL

Director: If we know the mechanism of the soul, we can manipulate it accordingly.

Woman: Our own soul or the souls of others? Either way, I think there's truth to what you say. What do we call soul manipulators?

Director: Priests.

Woman: Yes, but you and I aren't priests and we would have this knowledge.

Director: Maybe it's bad knowledge to have.

Woman: Imprudent knowledge? Only if we get caught.

Director: Please don't make me laugh. It's not appropriate to the scene. But who's to catch us? The one we manipulate?

Woman: Well, of course they would know.

Director: Would they? Maybe not. They might think it was all their idea.

Woman: I don't know, Director. I think they would know. Besides, it's kind of creepy to manipulate from behind the scene.

Director: Behind the scene or behind the soul? What is the soul?

Woman: It's the combination of heart and mind into spirit.

Director: That's a neat definition. And we can have high spirits and low spirits, yes?

Woman: We certainly can.

Director: Are high spirits always comfortable?

Woman: They're not uncomfortable. They're a feeling we like to have.

Director: Ascetics don't like them. They don't trust them. And I think they have some sense in this.

Woman: You prefer low spirits?

Director: I prefer steady spirits—not too high, not too low. Everyone crows about high spirits. I don't. I'll side with the ascetics on this.

Woman: You're worried you'll lose your judgement if you get too high? Or maybe you're worried about the great comedown?

Director: It's not really worry. It's doubt born of experience. Do you often experience high spirits?

Woman: I get them often when I perform. They evaporate quickly afterwards.

Director: Do you feel down afterwards?

Woman: A little. But I build my spirits up toward the next performance. It takes work, you know.

Director: That's something people don't seem to get. It does take work to maintain your spirits. But people seem to think of it like the weather.

Woman: It's a little like the weather in that they're not wholly in our control. We can do things to influence them—work—but sometimes things come along that render it all for naught.

Director: And sometimes things come along that lift us up.

Woman: True. Do you resist if someone tries to lift you up?

Director: Oh yes, definitely. After all, to try is not to succeed.

Woman: But this is important. If someone could lift you up, would you let them?

Director: What do we mean by up? Are we speaking of elevating the soul? Or are we talking about making us giddy for a time?

Woman: Take your pick. But I would choose elevation any time. You would, too.

Director: What does it mean to be elevated in soul?

Woman: To be worthy in feeling and thought.

Director: Not thought and feeling? Which comes first?

Woman: The chicken or the egg? Thoughts beget feelings, and feelings beget thoughts. They're of a piece.

Director: So if I only think hard enough I can feel good, elevated?

Woman: You're raising too many questions. Are goodness and elevation one? That's something I'd rather know first.

Director: The answer is no, they're not the same. Today's virtue is a low and solid thing, not high and dicey as in the past.

THOUGHT

Woman: So I caught you in a lie. You tried to sneak your equation of goodness and elevation by me without an explanation.

Director: If we have to explain everything, where will we be?

Woman: You're the philosopher. You should tell me. So what happens if goodness and elevation are one?

Director: The times will change.

Woman: So that's all philosophy has to do? Aim lower or higher and the world moves?

Director: That's what some philosophers think. I don't. I'm not in control of the world. I'm not even in control of my own little world, struggle as I might.

Woman: Do you think those philosophers find comfort in believing they move the world? Does it make all of their effort seem worthwhile?

Director: It's a very tempting thought, I can tell you. Who wants to struggle for no reason?

Woman: But you're only *tempted* to think that way. And have a purpose, even though I might not know what it is.

Director: Yes, but we need to emphasize the temptation. It starts out in the form of philosophy's own chicken and egg question. Which came first? The change in the world or the change in our thought?

Woman: You mean philosophers might simply notice a change before others.

Director: Yes, and to me that's a win—though it comes at a cost.

Woman: Aside from megalomania, why do some philosophers believe their thought causes the change in the world?

Director: Sometimes I think philosophers believe this in order to stay sane.

Woman: What if it's a combination of the two? There is a change in the world; philosophers notice it first; then they seek to influence the way things turn out.

Director: You've hit remarkably close to my own view. Interpretation of the change can influence events.

Woman: But that's awful. I mean, we all need to interpret the world on our own, if we're to be true. Along comes a philosopher and says, 'Look, there's a great change coming our way. This is what it means.' But this allows the other to effectively ignore the change and its meaning and take it on trust.

Director: That frees the other to act. He or she isn't crippled in exhaustive interpretation.

Woman: The other is freed from thought. I thought you wanted to stir thought, you liar.

Director: I'm glad you said that with a smile. Some of us don't need to think.

Woman: Ha! Says the philosopher. Why on earth not?

Director: What is thought?

Woman: What is comfort? What is soul? What is thought? You are the king of *what is*. Thought? It's the digestion of facts.

Director: You read that somewhere, didn't you? In some philosopher's collected works?

Woman: Thought doesn't need to be original in order to be true.

Director: There *is* some healthy truth in that, even if it's false.

Woman: So now you're going to tell me truth and originality are one?

Director: I am.

Woman: So your thoughtless drones who change the world, what original truth have they got?

Director: That's something they discover as they go.

Woman: Don't they share?

Director: No. After all, what's to share if there's no thought?

Woman: I don't like this. You sound as if you enter into some sort of understanding with these drones, and you and they go on to tear a path through the world.

Director: What's wrong with opening a way that others follow? Or would you have us all clear our own way? Do you believe everyone is capable of opening a way? If not, where would they be if not for thought-less drones?

Woman: But you don't call them drones to their faces.

Director: I call them much worse. And do you know what they do? They laugh! They think I'm the fool for sharing what I know.

Woman: What, no gratitude?

Director: For what? And no, there is none here.

WAITING

Woman: Does gratitude leave you with a bad taste in your mouth?

Director: It does. Do you know why? It's because gratitude always wants to be repaid.

Woman: What kind of nonsense it that? Gratitude wants to pay its debt.

Director: And be repaid in reputation as one who pays their debt.

Woman: You sometimes seem more like a flim flam man than philosopher, you know.

Director: That's all part of my plan.

Woman: Do tell.

Director: If my *drones* think I'm a flim flam man, they won't be obliged to feel like they owe me anything. And I really don't want anything from them—least of all that they be drones. I want them to think self-contained thoughts, not to be overwhelmed by the changes in the world. And out of this isolation they will do great things.

Woman: So you're like a sort of twisted mother, in the end.

Director: You continue to unriddle me, Woman. But *sort of* is only sort of. I'm no mother to them.

Woman: Are you a father?

Director: No. I am someone who waits. I wait to see what the world wants.

Woman: And when you do?

Director: Sometimes I comply; sometimes I resist. And to my *drones* I'm a sort of bellwether this way.

Woman: Your drones are sheep?

Director: No. This is very hard, if not impossible, to explain.

Woman: Am I a drone?

Director: Not even a *sort* of drone.

Woman: What are you waiting for from me?

Director: You and I are stuck here waiting together for news of our friends.

Woman: Thanks for reminding me. But if we weren't stuck? Would we be friends?

Director: If I weren't me and you weren't you; and the world were other than it is.... What's the point of speculating here? We are here. That's a fact. Digest it if you can.

Woman: Can you?

Director: I'm working on it as we speak.

Woman: Give me your phone number now. I don't want us out of joy or sorrow not to connect.

Director: Here. Now please, may I have yours?

Woman: Take it. Who will call first?

Director: I don't know. Does it matter?

Woman: We were put here today for a reason. That's what I believe. Every-thing happens for a reason.

Director: Sometimes it happens just from luck.

Woman: No, there is a reason in everything. That's what I believe.

Director: I think you believe something else. I think you believe that if you *apply* reason to everything, you can achieve good things. Is that what you believe?

Woman: It's a choice between reason happening to us, and us using reason. I prefer to think we use reason, as you suggest. Otherwise we just sit around and wait.

Director: Waiting, yes. The favorite game of many. They wait and interpret the signs according to whatever voodoo philosophy they espouse. Never once do they take a decisive step.

Woman: And philosophy is in the business of taking decisive steps?

Director: We can take steps in our thought. And this prepares us to take steps—

Woman: —in real life?

Director: That's not what I was going to say.

LIFE

Woman: I don't care what you were going to say. Let's talk about thought and real life.

Director: Thought *is* real life. Isn't it?

Woman: You know that's not true. I've heard it said. Steps forward in thought are the only true steps in life. Everything follows from them. Well, what if that's not true? What if thought is the laggard? What if thought is making up for life?

Director: Ah, you've shot an arrow through my heart. Just kidding. So what if thought is second to *life*? I still think thought is worth it.

Woman: So do I. But what is life?

Director: What is comfort? What is soul? What is thought? What is life? What is, what is, what is. I don't know. What is life?

Woman: Life is the living. The feeling. The urging. The terror. The joy. It is all. And I want it that way.

Director: You're a woman of excellent taste. But you didn't mention thought in your litany. Don't you want that, too?

Woman: I do. But I can't help but feel that all these other things come first. It's only when we have quiet from all this that we can think.

Director: True. But once we've thought we experience these other things differently. Or hasn't that been your experience?

Woman: Are you asking if I haven't thought? Or are you asking if I haven't *profited* from my thought?

Director: Who says experiencing things differently is *profit*? What if you find comfort in your thought and the new experiences it brings? Profit? Is comfort profit?

Woman: People would pay lots of good money for comfort. So comfort can *bring* profit, I suppose.

Director: But that's not how you see it, is it? As you said, life is the living. Living is more important than profiting.

Woman: What does that mean for comfort? Isn't comfort part of life? Or does comfort *allow* for life?

Director: That's an interesting question. What's the character of our living when we are in great discomfort? Can we be said to be living then?

Woman: We live. But we store up our experiences for digestion at another time, a time when comfort allows us to think.

Director: But don't we need to be able to think when we're uncomfortable? Isn't that what allows us to escape to a place of comfort?

Woman: Escape. I didn't have you pegged as an escapist. But we do need to escape discomfort, great discomfort, if we can.

Director: A little discomfort is okay? We can think when we're lightly discomforted?

Woman: A little is okay. I'd say it even makes us more alive. It spurs us on. It makes us think.

Director: Makes us think? And what's this? Are you equating life with thought? I never thought I'd see the day.

Woman: Based on our long relationship, no—who would have thought? And no, I don't equate life with thought. But they should complement one another. After all, isn't that what we've been saying?

Director: We have, if not in so many words.

Woman: Yes in so many, many words! I don't recall ever having talked so much in my life! Is that what philosophy does? It makes us run at the mouth?

Director: Some people it shuts right up. Who can say why? But how do you know it's philosophy and not just the circumstances we're under?

Woman: I think I have the answer to why it shuts some people up. You strike me as someone who won't put up with pretensions. Pretenders, when confronted with truth, grow quiet.

Director: But we need to be careful here. There are others who grow quiet that we mustn't confuse with pretenders.

Woman: What kind of people are they?

Director: The kind that are very much alive.

QUIET

Woman: How can we recognize these people?

Director: For one, they weren't pretending... very much.

Woman: Do you think we all pretend a little? Philosophers included?

Director: If so, philosophers pretend very little—maybe just enough to get by.

Woman: And they always feel remorse for having sinned?

Director: No. They act out of necessity. Sometimes we *have* to pretend.

Woman: Let's have an example.

Director: Maybe another time.

Woman: Oh, I hit a nerve! Then I'll give an example. A philosopher will pretend to take an interest in someone he's stuck with—because otherwise he'd be a churl.

Director: That *otherwise* isn't a necessity. It may be prudent, to keep up a decent reputation, for instance. But necessary? No. A pretension is a sort of lie. What's necessary is the truth. When lie meets truth the lie is forgiven.

Woman: Why can't truth meet truth?

Director: Because sometimes too much truth can kill.

Woman: The truth is a powerful thing. But why lie? Why not maintain silence when confronted with a terrible truth?

Director: That takes lots of strength. It *uses* lots of strength. Sometimes strength is better spent elsewhere.

Woman: You have an answer for everything, don't you?

Director: Sometimes I'm very quiet, not many answers at all. It's either that or play the buffoon. My character bristles at being a buffoon. I know others who can pull it off. How about you? Are you a quiet violinist?

Woman: I am. I say hardly a word to anyone at work. Even with my friends I'm quiet and shy.

Director: When I'm quiet I'm not shy. My eyes give me away. People take my silence as arrogance. But that's not how they take you.

Woman: How do you know?

Director: I see how your eyes are now. So I can imagine how they are then.

Woman: You don't strike me as... very much arrogant!

Director: You're funny. I know I'm not arrogant. Arrogance is when you have too high an opinion of yourself. My opinion, if anything, is probably low.

Woman: And that's not arrogant thing to say! Ha, ha. Why do you think my eyes are different than yours?

Director: You're more sensitive than I am.

Woman: You strike me as very sensitive.

Director: I mean, you care too much about the feelings of others. You're afraid your eyes would sear their souls if left free to gaze as they would.

Woman: I do fear that. But more—I fear retaliation.

Director: So do I. I'm no fool, you know. And so I break my silence and talk when it comes to that point.

Woman: What do you say?

Director: Things to distract from my eyes.

Woman: You don't avert your eyes. You say something instead. I wish I could do that.

Director: It takes a little practice. And you'll get a reputation you might not like. But I think it's worth a try.

Woman: I'd rather put myself in situations where silence is fine. Like work. I let my violin speak.

Director: I'm sure it gives great expression to your spirit—even if the music is bad. There's something about something bad being played with verve.

Woman: You should come to hear me play sometime.

Director: I would like that. Do you ever play Telemann?

Woman: Not at work, no. He's not in vogue. But I do play in a pickup quartet that performs his Paris pieces. Strictly an amateur thing.

Director: The *Quadri* and *Nouveaux Quatuors*?

Woman: You know them that well!

Director: It's one thing to know a name, another to know the score. And I like amateurs best.

Amateur

Woman: Why amateurs?

Director: It's simple. I'm more comfortable with them. And you?

Woman: I am, too. There's no money involved. I like the freedom in that. We can play what we like. We don't owe anyone anything.

Director: I find that amateurs are less jaded, more naturally enthusiastic. But usually not as good. Somehow I think your amateurs will be great.

Woman: I'm going to circulate the scores and we'll play for you in a month!

Director: A private audience?

Woman: Ha, ha. No, not quite. We play at a small museum once a month for free. It's a sort of charitable donation. I feel very comfortable there.

Director: You don't feel comfortable on the main stage? You're first chair. If you can't be comfortable, who can?

Woman: There's a lot of pressure on me. There is no pressure at the museum. Do you think some people are comfortable with pressure?

Director: A certain amount of pressure, yes. I do think there is a limit, though. Some people with pressure-comfort keep pushing things to know where the limit is at.

Woman: They really want to know? It's not enough to feel comfortable where most others are anything but? I really can't relate. What if they don't find a limit? What happens then?

Director: They live a truly blessed life.

Woman: How rare do you think that is?

Director: A handful every thousand years—that we know about.

Woman: We only know the famous.

Director: Right. If you're a professional, say. But how many amateurs are there in the world? How many feel so little discomfort with pressure—whatever kind of pressure—that it gets them killed?

Woman: Discomfort is a warning sign. That makes sense. But no one is going to kill the first chair violin. So what's *my* discomfort for? What's it warning me off?

Director: I don't know. Maybe if I came to see a concert I'd find a clue. You really don't know? Maybe it's telling you to find another job.

Woman: I can't imagine what I'd do. Sell insurance?

Director: You could teach music.

Woman: Ah. I would like that I think, very much. But what if I'm uncomfortable in that?

Director: As first chair violin don't you teach the other violinists what to do?

Woman: I do. But it's collaborative, really.

Director: Students can collaborate with the teacher. Does collaboration make you uneasy?

Woman: Sometimes it does. If they don't play well it's seen as my fault. It *is* my fault.

Director: Maybe up to a point. You'll have some bad students. It won't be your fault. Are you one of these people who thinks everything is their fault?

Woman: I believe what happens in life depends on me.

Director: Yes, that's admirable—up to a point. You have to be realistic here. Not everything is your fault.

Woman: I didn't know you were a therapist. What are we talking about anyway? A job. But we're agreed amateurs are best.

Director: Can you afford not to have a job?

Woman: Yes. I could teach for free. And play in my pickup quartet.

Director: Would you be happy? Would you miss your orchestra performances?

Woman: I would. I should have told you. There is a lot of pressure. And it makes me uncomfortable. But when I'm really playing well, which is most of the time, I forget the pressure and am one with the music.

Director: The pressure is before you start.

Woman: Always. I wouldn't miss that. I'd miss the high. No amateur performance can ever take me there. I love the free performances, but not like I love the main stage.

Acting

Director: When you perform, do you act?

Woman: What, you mean do I fake passion? No!

Director: Do others?

Woman: Yes. And it's an awful thing. I can't stand playing with people like that. The passion must be pure—or the music suffers.

Director: If you were to listen to a recording of a concert, could you tell if there were phonies in the orchestra?

Woman: Yes. The music wouldn't gel. If you were reading a book of philosophy, could you tell where the author was faking?

Director: Some fake better than others—but yes. Do you think some musicians are comfortable when they act?

Woman: Are some philosophers comfortable when they lie? I think the answer is yes, in both cases.

Director: Yet you are not.

Woman: And you are not. Why? What makes us different than the others?

Director: Maybe we just want that pure feeling of the truth. But what do you do if you're just not feeling the music for some reason? Do you get up and leave in the middle of a performance?

Woman: You know that's not possible. It's a problem. What about you? If you're not feeling the reason, do you just fold up your tent and go?

Director: Yes, I do. Philosophy has an advantage here. If I'm talking to someone I can excuse myself and walk away. If I'm writing an essay, I can just get up and walk away—and even delete what I had written.

Woman: Are you more comfortable talking or writing?

Director: What's your guess?

Woman: Well, you're quite the talker. But I would guess writing, because you can delete.

Director: Not once you've committed by sharing your work.

Woman: True. But talking doesn't let you edit your words. I think there's more pressure here. I once knew an author of beautiful works who spoke like he never made it past tenth grade.

Director: Was he nervous? Sometimes that's the thing. A nervous speaker can certainly be a beautiful writer. There's no contradiction there.

Woman: And a powerful speaker may be a terrible writer.

Director: Can a wonderful musician be an awful composer?

Woman: Of course! It happens all the time. And wonderful composers can be awful musicians—in a technical sense, of course.

Director: But I can't help but think about you on the stage, not feeling the music but having to play. You're forced to fake it, to act. I'm never forced that way.

Woman: Never? I seem to recall your having said we're all sometimes forced to act, to pretend, to lie—out of necessity.

Director: Did I say that? Here, let me edit the book.

Woman: Ha! So which version of the truth is true?

Director: Whichever version you please.

Woman: Hmm. What are my choices? I get the perfect version of you, or the human version of you. I'll take the human any day. Which philosophers do you prefer? The perfect or the human?

Director: The human, of course. Perfect philosophers are called theologians.

Woman: Speakers of God. I never thought of it that way, but I think you have a point. So what's your favorite philosophical flaw?

Director: That would be my own—which I'll leave to you to discover. Next best is the propensity to lie to prove a point.

Woman: So you've never lied to prove a point?

Director: I was speaking of propensities. But let me tell you why I like the argument by lie. It catches up the lazy, the ones not really following the argument well, the ones who don't verify what the philosopher says. I once knew a philosopher who led his followers on a wild goose chase. Bad inferences, with untrue examples and facts. I came into it after it had gone on for a number of years. There were so many untruths flying around I didn't know what to do.

Woman: What did you do?

Director: I made it clear to the philosopher that I saw the untruths—and left his students to him and his lies.

Woman: Why didn't you clear things up?

Director: To what end? And could I really have cleared things up once they had gotten so dirty? Not my mess to clean.

Woman: Why would a philosopher do that? And what exactly was he doing?

Director: Exactly? He was pretending to believe what he was saying.

LIES

Woman: That's such a fundamental lie I don't know what to think. From a *philosopher* no less!

Director: Do you think philosophers are Boy Scouts? Honest as the day is long?

Woman: No. Yes! Shouldn't they be? I thought they cared about truth. I thought they were only comfortable with truth.

Director: There are many uncomfortable truths. Lying philosophers are one.

Woman: So what does this mean?

Director: You can't just take what philosophers say on trust.

Woman: Then they're like anyone else.

Director: Not quite. When you examine what they say you'll sometimes find the truth in the lie. The purpose of the lie. With this purpose you forgive. And you learn something, too.

Woman: What do you learn? When you should lie yourself? When lies are as good as truth? When lies are better than truth?

Director: You learn to lie to defend the truth. You learn to lie to defend yourself. And to have a little fun.

Woman: You're comfortable with that? Lying for fun?

Director: Would it help if I told you it's fine so long as no one gets hurt?

Woman: The followers on the goose chase don't get hurt?

Director: No, they don't. They might be embarrassed once the truth is known. But hurt? Hardly. You'd have to know these people to see what I mean. A little embarrassment might slow them down and urge them to think.

Woman: So thinking being good, good comes of the lie.

Director: Would it help if I told you that that philosopher spent years trying very patiently to show them the truth—and they wouldn't listen? So he took another tack.

Woman: That does help. I'm a little more comfortable with the idea. But how will they find out the truth? What if they never learn?

Director: He's going to just get more and more wild until they'll be forced to reject what he says.

Woman: Why philosophize with people like that?

Director: He loves them.

Woman: What! Why would he love people who won't listen to truth?

Director: He teaches a truth that's hard to swallow. He knows this. He doesn't see any other choice.

Woman: So he amuses himself with his outrageous lies.

Director: Yes. It's compensation for all his hard work—and not without irony, too.

Woman: Why irony? Is he playing dumb?

Director: Yes, certainly. But also irony in the conventional sense. He came to know enough to know how to lie in this case by being very honest with himself.

Woman: I'd like to meet your philosopher friend.

Director: Maybe one day you will.

Woman: He's intriguing. What's his biggest lie?

Director: That philosophers make the world go round.

Woman: We've talked about this. But how do I know *you're* not lying here? What if they *do* make the world go round, and you know this; but you're lying to me by saying they don't.

Director: Why would I lie about that?

Woman: Because for the scheme to work, philosophers must be covert actors. Otherwise, who would listen to them?

Director: Oh no.

Woman: Oh no, what?

Director: It's happening again.

Woman: What's wrong?

Director: Philosophy is being accused of terrible things.

Woman: Why terrible things?

Director: Because that's what makes the world go round.

TERRIBLE

Woman: I thought you might say love makes the world go round.

Director: Love running away from terrible things. But then again, that might be a lie. Love itself can be a terrible thing.

Woman: How so? Love makes life worth living. Or are you talking about pent up unrequited love? I agree—that's a terrible thing. But why would it make the world go round?

Director: Imagine a cartoon globe that moves under our running feet like a treadmill. The lover runs toward the beloved; the beloved runs away. Neither goes anywhere; they just stay in place; but they exhaust themselves, nonetheless.

Woman: What does philosophy do about the situation?

Director: It plants one foot firmly on the moon, and with the other it stops the spinning globe. Philosophy doesn't make the world go round. It stops the world from going round.

Woman: Why would it do that? To end the chase? To help free the beloved? To make the lover wake up and realize the folly of the love?

Director: No. It would do it because it *can*.

Woman: Let me get this straight. Philosophy would stop the world spinning because of a whim? No I think you're lying to me.

Director: Why?

Woman: You strike me as more serious than that.

Director: The serious need their whims in order to stay sane. Don't you have any whims? You strike me as the serious type.

Woman: I haven't been very serious with you today.

Director: Maybe. But I can tell that's the exception. Serious is the rule. Are you uncomfortable with being called what you are?

Woman: No. But I don't *want* to be serious. It just works out that way. It's a sort of self-defense.

Director: No one gets your jokes.

Woman: It's true! They all joke in their own way. They feel free to joke. I don't. Once in a great while I'll out with something very funny. So they know I'm alive. But it's certainly not the rule.

Director: Does it make you feel terrible to have to be that way? To keep your personality submerged?

Woman: Yes. But what should I do? Play the clown? I can't see any other way.

Director: I don't know, Woman. It's hard to say you should play the clown. For one, you have no practice, and you might fall and break a leg.

Woman: Do you have practice playing the clown?

Director: I do. A long time ago. Before I found my philosophical feet.

Woman: That was when you first learned to stop the world. That must have been a terrible thing.

Director: I was comfortable with the world stopped. It made me feel good.

Woman: You mean it made you feel a way you liked. That way might not have been good. After all, when you stop the world you kill everything that grows.

Director: How so?

Woman: The sun. It shines only on one part of the world when it's stopped. That part burns up. The other parts wither away.

Director: Yes, but the day is long. Many things can be done before the killing starts. And then I lift my foot and it spins again, bringing darkness and light where needed.

A Touch

Woman: You don't really believe all that. I can tell. Maybe there's a touch of truth in there. But on the whole? It's a lie.

Director: Can't I tell the truth but not believe that truth?

Woman: Why would you do that?

Director: To protect myself from being burned up by the sun.

Woman: You would really speak truth but not believe it? That sounds... crazy!

Director: Stranger things have happened. After all, people speak lies and believe them all the time.

Woman: Yes, but that's natural. What you're suggesting is unnatural.

Director: Why?

Woman: Because if you don't believe the truth, why would you bother to speak it?

Director: Because I want others to believe it.

Woman: Why?

Director: They grow healthier that way.

Woman: And you would be sick? Is that what you want? I don't think so. I sense a great health in you.

Director: I can afford not to believe the truth.

Woman: So does that make you a liar who speaks truth?

Director: Yes.

Woman: I'm not impressed.

Director: I'm not trying to impress you. I'm trying to tell you the truth.

Woman: Your crazy truth. But I don't believe it. You're teasing about the difference between believing and knowing. You don't *believe* the truth, yes—because you *know* it.

Director: Very good. That might be true. I'll have to give it some thought.

Woman: Now you're pretending not to know that it's true.

Director: There's a touch of truth in everything we say. Is that true?

Woman: True of us—you and me? Or true of us—all humanity?

Director: Does it make a difference? Let's say it's all humanity. Are we being generous? A touch of truth in everything that everyone says. That's generous.

Woman: But it's hard to be completely false. You'd really have to try.

Director: Partly true takes no effort. Truly false takes great effort. What about completely true? Great effort or impossibility?

Woman: I think it's impossible to be completely false, just as it's impossible to be completely true.

Director: So there's a touch of darkness and light in everything we say.

Woman: In some there's much more than a touch. But what if there were only a touch of light and only a touch of darkness. What would be the rest?

Director: Empty filler. We have to avoid people with that.

Woman: But not avoid someone who is almost completely dark? I don't know, Director. I find all of this very hard to believe. Yes, there is darkness and light. And yes, there is empty filler. But somehow I feel like our conversation is drifting into dangerous waters.

Director: Drifting? I take your point. Sometimes empty filler is good. It comforts us. We don't have to work to understand. There's nothing to understand. It's just white noise that drowns out the rest. What's wrong with that?

Woman: There's nothing wrong with that. And yet I hate talking to those who speak empty filler. I can't make chit chat to save my life.

Director: Yes, but you have your violin. I don't have anything to shield me from the need to converse.

Woman: You speak emptiness now and then?

Director: I speak emptiness and I rest. When speaking to the empty, give them what they are. That's what I say.

Woman: But you try to get away from them?

Director: As often as I can. But I don't get many vacations in this life.

Woman: How do you do it? How do you carry on?

Director: I live for the moments when I can speak falseness or truth.

Woman: You live for the moments when you can speak truth—not falseness, Director.

Director: Falseness excites. What can I say?

Woman: But who deserves the false?

Director: Are you looking for justice? Giving each what they deserve? So who deserves the false? Those who can appreciate it for what it is.

FALSEHOOD

Woman: Tell me how that looks.

Director: Let's say a boor comes up and sits down next to us here. He muscles his way into our conversation. He asks what we were talking about. I tell him we were talking about how uncomfortable these chairs are. That's false. We mentioned that they are hard, but that was about it. Yet I make it sound like our conversation has been one of complaint.

Woman: Well, yes—that's untrue. But does that really excite?

Director: Me? Not really. It's the next step that excites.

Woman: What step?

Director: I tell him, by way of complaint, that we finally succeeded in driving off a boor who sat exactly where he's sitting now. I complain there are so many boors. Doesn't he agree?

Woman: You sound like you're picking a fight.

Director: But I do it in a very gentle voice. And we might be surprised. 'Yes,' he says, 'there are very many boors. I can't stand a boor.' And he tells us his experience. Surprise is exciting, no? And who knows what he might say?

Woman: If you find boors complaining about boors exciting, what can I say?

Director: Did he deserve the truth? Should we tell him about lying philosophers and all such things? About being uncomfortable in first chair but loving the highs when they come? Shall we be completely truthful with him?

Woman: No, of course not.

Director: And if he won't take silence as a hint?

Woman: But even if he does, his just being there inhibits our conversation. We can't speak freely any longer.

Director: Then we can amuse ourselves by speaking great big lies for him to hear.

Woman: I don't know. That sounds like trouble. I know we'll never see him again—but maybe we will. What then?

Director: Ah, it's prudence versus amusement. A true philosophical dilemma. We can cut the Gordian knot by getting up and sitting somewhere else.

Woman: But that's rude. He'll likely take offense.

Director: Who, some boor? So what? Are you that afraid of giving offense that you'd sacrifice our free conversation?

Woman: But even then it wouldn't be free. I'd feel his resentment from across the room. I'm sensitive like that, as you said.

Director: So successful conversation with you depends on luck. A little bit of bad luck, the appearance of a boor, can't be overcome. What if we stand up, politely excuse ourselves, and say we'd like some privacy to discuss private things? Then we move to the other side of the room.

Woman: That would be better. That would be good.

Director: Why?

Woman: Because we're treating him with respect.

Director: Are we treating him with respect because he deserves respect, or because we're afraid?

Woman: Because... we're afraid.

Director: What makes us afraid? Why fear a boor?

Woman: We don't know who this man is. He might make trouble for us.

Director: He already has.

Woman: Yes, but you know what I mean. Real trouble. Trouble we don't need.

Director: Maybe that's all respect is—polite behavior driven by fear.

Woman: No, that's not all respect is. I respect my father. I'm not afraid of him. He's the sweetest man in the world.

Director: You have a point. Maybe some respect is driven by fear and some respect is driven by love. Are you comfortable with that?

Woman: I am. I think it's true. But it's no good for the two to meet.

Director: What do you mean?

Woman: Let's suppose we're dealing with the bore respectfully, and along comes my father. The boor sees a different sort of respect in play. And it bothers him.

Director: He wants the respect of love.

Woman: Yes. And that's something you can't fake.

RESPECT

Director: But in all honesty, I would never attempt to fake the respect of love. Would you?

Woman: Never.

Director: Do you say that on moral grounds? Or because it can't be done?

Woman: What difference does it make? I wouldn't make the attempt.

Director: Not even if your life depended on it?

Woman: Not even then. Look, let's say I could fool someone with this. I would only be making a prison for myself. I'd have to keep up the act.

Director: Or show your contempt. Yes, I see what you mean.

Woman: What's your reason not to fake this respect?

Director: It's similar to yours. It buys you nothing and you can't win. So why do it?

Woman: Cowardice is why. You're afraid to let someone know you don't respect them the way they want.

Director: If you don't respect them the way they want, does that mean you have no respect for them at all?

Woman: Well, we'd be talking about the respect of fear. But someone who's not satisfied with that, someone who wants more, would raise my contempt. I don't respect, even out of fear, those for whom I have contempt.

Director: I don't think the respect of fear is good.

Woman: Of course it's not good! It's necessary, though.

Director: I think we should fight this respect when we see it.

Woman: What, disrupt others' lives? That's a cruel thing to do.

Director: The one demanding respect is much crueler, don't you think? And doesn't he or she disrupt others' lives more? I'd do away with the respect of fear.

Woman: How about the respect of prudence?

Director: Ah, you ask a good question. Fear and prudence are linked. I vote in favor of the respect of prudence, but not the respect of fear. A sort of compromise, if you will.

Woman: What if the respect of prudence is more cowardly than the respect of fear?

Director: Can you say more?

Woman: The respect of fear is defensive in nature. The respect of prudence might be defensive—but it can also be looking for advantage.

Director: What's wrong with looking for advantage? How else do you think we can win?

Woman: It's not about winning.

Director: What's it about?

Woman: It's not about petty advantage. Petty prudence. Pathetic prudence. Prudence, prudence, prudence—even the word sounds lame.

Director: What if it were about grand advantage—and we called it something else?

Woman: Give an example of grand advantage.

Director: Statesmen lying to one another.

Woman: Statesmen? I've met enough politicians to know there are no statesmen left. It's all grubbing for money or fame.

Director: I'm not sure I've ever heard someone speak of grubbing for fame. What's wrong with fame?

Woman: There's nothing wrong with fame. I have a little fame, you know. I appear often enough as one of the faces of the orchestra, along with the conductor. But I didn't ask for this fame. I *earned* this fame. And I didn't get it by respecting the lame.

Director: Your orchestra, it has a board?

Woman: Most orchestras do, yes. What's your point? I'm curious to know.

Director: Have you met the board members?

Woman: I have.

Director: Where?

Woman: You know where.

Director: At fundraisers.

Woman: Don't you even say it. I don't engage in grubbing for donations.

Director: Of course you don't. You're a star. Stars just have to... be. And by simply being themselves they gain respect.

Woman: Don't you care about *your* respect?

Director: I do and I don't. I'm aware that you can't be utterly contemptible to most. But I don't care when it comes to some.

Woman: Which some?

Director: Those who don't deserve respect.

Woman: You're such a liar! You think most people don't deserve respect. Am I wrong?

Director: Some, most; many, few—who's to say? I haven't done the math to tell you for sure. It's just some people don't deserve respect. And some of those *some* view me as contemptible for speaking cold truth.

CONTEMPT

Woman: Contempt is comfortable, isn't it?

Director: More comfortable than facing up to the truth. But let's hold on a minute. There might be a virtue to contempt.

Woman: What virtue? Contempt is a riled up state of soul. How can there be virtue there?

Director: Contempt creates distance.

Woman: You mean the contemptuous think they're above.

Director: Maybe. But I was thinking of lateral distance. Distance as in getting away. Getting away from the grubbers, whatever they're grubbing for. Distance as in retreating to a lake in the woods, far from the maddening crowd.

Woman: If contempt could bring me to a lake house beyond the woods, I would be so contemptuous you couldn't believe.

Director: But I can believe it. I certainly can. Contempt is a way of standing alone. Who shares contempt?

Woman: That's a good question. I'm not sure anyone does. Maybe a mother could teach her cubs content for certain types of people? Grubbers and the like?

Director: Yes, but cubs don't always learn the lessons they're supposed to learn. They learn—they certainly do. But not what they were taught, all the time.

Woman: That's true. Contempt is a solo endeavor. And when I think of the house by the lake near the woods—I think of myself alone.

Director: Do you have contempt for your board?

Woman: How could I and still show up to work?

Director: You'd just have to sink your roots deeper.

Woman: What roots?

Director: You don't have roots under your chair?

Woman: How could I? I could lose that chair any season. And not because of lack of merit.

Director: Politics? Do you have contempt for politics?

Woman: I do. And you?

Director: Politics are fun.

Woman: Ha! You really are such a liar.

Director: But I only lie for fun. A friend of mine once wrote a book about *the lie.* That was his conclusion. You can only lie for fun—so long as no one gets hurt.

Woman: Sounds like a sensible man. But when you lie of necessity, are you having fun?

Director: Necessity can be so much fun—depending who you are.

Woman: What does that mean? Who has fun with terrible necessity? And don't say *me!*

Director: I'm not sure if *me* means Woman or Director. Either way, I think both of us can have fun. Necessity is truly terrible only when we aren't willing to lie.

Woman: Oh, that's not true at all. True necessity couldn't care less whether we tell the truth or lie.

Director: Maybe not, but those who wash up on the shore with the waves of necessity very much care. We'd like to drive them back off the beach. Back to where they came.

Woman: As if our words had so much power.

Director: You hold words in contempt? I didn't know this about you. I thought you were a word-serious girl.

Woman: And you're a sometimes serious wordy guy.

Director: I'll take that as just. Thank you.

Woman: There is no need to thank someone for justice, you know. Justice does good to the doer.

Director: I don't doubt it does. Are you always serious? I think it's possible you are, except for now with me.

Woman: I'll confess, I'm mostly serious, yes.

Director: What about your friends?

Woman: They're serious, too.

Director: No, this is a shame. I think you should spend time with me and learn to play.

Woman: Isn't that exactly what I've been doing today? But I fear it's not appropriate.

Director: Because of our friends.

Woman: Yes. Their lives hang in the balance.

Director: Nothing we do or say out here will influence their cause in either way. Or are you uncomfortable with that?

JINX

Woman: We might jinx the operations.

Director: You *are* uncomfortable with that. Bad luck, yes. You're more pious than I knew.

Woman: Pious?

Director: Piety brings on good luck. Didn't you know?

Woman: What is piety? I'd like to hear you say.

Director: In your case? It's reverence. Serious concern for luck. Serious fear not to jinx, as if you were somehow responsible if the surgeon slips.

Woman: Don't talk like that.

Director: You don't think surgeons sometimes slip?

Woman: Stop! I thought you were a sensitive man.

Director: I am. I'm sensitive to you, to your not feeling like it's your fault if things don't turn out well. That's a very real risk with you. I'd rather have you have a low opinion of me than blame yourself for something out your control.

Woman: I don't have a low opinion of you. I just worry too much, is all. It's taking so *long.*

Director: They're probably only half way done. We've been talking a while. Maybe I should go and find another chair.

Woman: No. You're right. We should be free to pass the time however we like. Nothing we do or say here affects things in there. I don't believe in a jinx.

Director: Many people believe in jinxes. I don't know why. Do they believe their inner state controls what happens out here?

Woman: I think they do. I think they believe God knows what they are thinking, and if their thoughts aren't pure—God will punish them.

Director: Do you believe God knows what you are thinking?

Woman: I don't. I used to, for a long time. But now I don't.

Director: Why not? Were you impious and suffered no harm?

Woman: I was pure and rewarded with no good.

Director: Some would say that's a test.

Woman: I don't believe anyone is testing me—other than you.

Director: Are you an atheist?

Woman: Are you?

Director: I don't believe in God. Do you?

Woman: I... don't.

Director: That used to be the biggest jinx there is.

Woman: In many places it still is. The believers will ensure you have bad luck.

Director: But it's not really luck, is it.

Woman: No, it's all a human affair. It's *all* a human affair. And if my friend dies....

Director: You will have won another friend today. I know that's no compensation, but it is another friend.

Woman: Why do people believe in God?

Director: Some believe because they want to feel everything happens for a reason.

Woman: It doesn't, does it.

Director: No, not everything happens for a reason. Some things happen for a passion.

Woman: A passion is a reason. Everything is a reason. Reasons and feelings, aren't they the same?

Director: It's hard to say. I've given it some thought, but I don't know. If you're clever, all your passions can be reasons; and if you're honest, all your reasons can be passions. Who can say?

Woman: I thought maybe *you*. But maybe we can work it out together. So which would you prefer to come out on top? Passion or reason?

Director: I think it's wise to distance the two, laterally. I'd like to keep my passions and reasons apart. And bring them together scientifically. So I can know.

Woman: Science here might amount to torture. Are you willing to torture yourself in order to know?

Director: Better I than someone else.

KNOWLEDGE

Woman: You really are willing?

Director: It depends on *what* I want to know. We're not talking about curiosities. We're talking about things we *really* want to know.

Woman: Give me an example.

Director: Imagine one yourself.

Woman: That's... fair. I suppose I'd want to know if love is true.

Director: Yours or the other's?

Woman: Both. And I suppose you'd say if I'm willing to torture myself, I'd be willing to torture the other, my love. Well, it's true. I would.

Director: Can a relationship stand up to torture? Wouldn't it be ironic to learn you really do have love, but now the relationship is dead?

Woman: Maybe we employ little tortures here and there, torture that doesn't amount to much. Knowledge doesn't take big torture, does it? A little does the trick?

Director: Well, Francis Bacon said in 1620 that 'the nature of things betrays itself more readily under the vexations of art than in its natural freedom.' People interpreted that as a call to torture.

Woman: But vexation isn't necessarily torture.

Director: No, it's not.

Woman: It sounds like Bacon called for us to make nature uncomfortable and see what it would say.

Director: I think you can make your lover a little uncomfortable for a bit.

Woman: And I don't think you need to torture yourself in order to know yourself—your passions and reasons. You just need a little discomfort, a little vexation.

Director: Yes, the vexation of art. What do you think *art* means in this sense?

Woman: Cunning. You have to sneak up on your passions and reasons—catch them unaware.

Director: But doesn't cunning *derive* from passions and reasons? Isn't it the combination of the two that amounts to cunning?

Woman: Yes, but think of it like this. An individual might not be self-aware. Paired with an equal, the two of them together can explore their individuality—perhaps better than either could have done alone.

Director: So passion and reason are this couple. And with their cunning they approach one passion or reason alone, vex it—make it uncomfortable—and sweat out the truth.

Woman: Yes, that's how it's done. But I have to tell you. I've always thought self-knowledge is over-rated. Or maybe it's not over-rated; maybe it's best arrived at through knowledge of others.

Director: So we vex others to learn about them, and maybe this knowledge reflects on us as well?

Woman: Exactly. We have to turn out in order to learn within.

Director: Is it that self-knowledge is over-rated, or that people go about it the wrong way?

Woman: They go about it the wrong way. Learn without to know within—that's the way. Self-knowledge is a sort of afterthought.

Director: Some afterthought. But I wonder. Are we comfortable as we make others vexed?

Woman: Maybe with practice. You should know—this is what philosophers do. Are you comfortable as you vex?

Director: I have to be, if I'm to catch glimpses of the truth. If I myself am vexed, I'll likely miss out.

Woman: Your comfort serves a purpose.

Director: Everything in a philosopher serves a purpose. We put it all to use.

Use

Woman: Including others? Do philosophers put others to use?

Director: Yes, they do.

Woman: In order to know? Or for other things, too.

Director: For other things, too.

Woman: What do you use others for?

Director: Many things. What do you use others for?

Woman: Who says I use them?

Director: Don't you use the other violinists in the orchestra to make beautiful music?

Woman: Well, yes, in a sense.

Director: A sense certainly counts. I use people at work, especially those that report to me.

Woman: You're not a servant leader?

Director: At times I am. But, no, not as a rule. I use my direct reports in order to solve problems.

Woman: Work problems?

Director: Sometimes other problems, too.

Woman: Is that ethical?

Director: To solve problems? I think we can say it is.

Woman: No, to use work resources to solve non-work problems.

Director: All work is the same to a philosopher.

Woman: Then maybe philosophers shouldn't lead.

Director: Would it matter to you if I tell you that my team likes to be used?

Woman: No one likes to be used.

Director: You like to be used to play the score, don't you?

Woman: Yes, but I'm really not being used. I'm just doing my job.

Director: And sometimes you're used at fundraising events. Just doing your job?

Woman: Well, that's a little different.

Director: I ask my reports to do things that are just a little different, too. Unethical?

Woman: I don't know. I'd have to see them in action to say.

Director: Fair enough. But there are people who like to be used, to be put to good use.

Woman: Putting to good use is different than being used. So, Director, do you put your people to good use?

Director: I just put them to use. The goodness of it, like self-knowledge, is an afterthought.

Woman: You really don't care about good use? Or are you saying the adjective good is unnecessary here? Any use is good.

Director: I put them to uses that will help achieve my ends.

Woman: What about their ends?

Director: I'm sure they put others to uses that will help them achieve their ends, too.

Woman: So we're all putting each other to use?

Director: Yes, especially those who decry those who put others to use. They're often the biggest users of all.

Woman: But not in a good way.

Director: In a bad way.

Woman: Why in a bad way?

Director: Because they can't admit to themselves they are putting people to use. And if you can't admit this, how well can you lead the others in their use?

Woman: So it all comes down to how good a user you are.

Director: It all comes down to how effective we are in our use.

LEADERSHIP

Woman: Are you comfortable when you're being used? I assume you're used, aren't you? Like everyone else?

Director: Not like everyone else, though I am certainly used. And I'm comfortable if I'm allowed full scope.

Woman: Why aren't you used like everyone else?

Director: I enjoy being used. It gives me purpose. A strong leader will see this in me, and recognize my talent. He or she will see I should be free to act as I see fit. This will bring results.

Woman: You take your purpose from being used? I had thought you were a little more... noble than that.

Director: Work isn't my only purpose. I take purpose from many things. But work is something I have to do, so I like to have purpose if I can.

Woman: What about philosophy? Is that the main purpose of your life? How do you exercise philosophy at work?

Director: Philosophy is something I am. If being yourself is purpose, I have purpose here. As for work, I exercise philosophy every chance I get.

Woman: Do you get many chances?

Director: I make my chances, which means I have them as often as possible. I'm always making chances to the best of my ability.

Woman: Does your team respect that in you? Do they think you're a good leader?

Director: They are a large part of the chances I make. I think my chances make things interesting for them. Do they like being interested? I think they do.

Woman: So that's your leadership philosophy? Making things interesting?

Director: More gets done that way. And people enjoy the work. What's your leadership philosophy?

Woman: I just help the other violinists play the best they can. I guess that's not a strategy, really. But do we need a strategy in order to lead?

Director: Tell me, Woman. Is there a difference between philosophy and strategy?

Woman: A philosophy is a way of doing things in general; a strategy seems a little more targeted than that.

Director: And there is a difference between a philosopher and a strategist, right?

Woman: I think so.

Director: What is that difference?

Woman: It's.... I guess I don't know. Philosophers look for the truth.

Director: And strategists don't?

Woman: No, I suppose they'd have to, if they want to make a good strategy.

Director: What's a 'good' strategy? Is it one that succeeds? Is it one that gets you what you want?

Woman: It is. Then you'll ask what's a good philosophy? Is it one that succeeds? I guess so, but succeeds at what? Finding the truth? But truth is just the first stop along the way for a strategist. For philosophy it's the end.

Director: You've cleared up the difference between philosophy and strategy, it seems. But is it the end for the philosopher? Doesn't the philosopher have to take the next step?

Woman: What, and become a strategist with the truth he or she knows? The philosopher must transform into something else?

Director: Maybe. And even as a strategist, once the strategy is clear, doesn't the philosopher-strategist have to become someone who will execute the strategy? An executive?

Woman: The executive uses people, right? So how is the philosopher-strategist-executive different from a simple executive?

Director: A simple executive isn't backed by personal strategy and truth. Those personal things belong to someone else. Surely it's an advantage to have your own, no?

Your Own

Woman: Yes, but we're being a little ridiculous. Of course an executive can have his or her own strategy and truth. And even if not, they can *make* these things their own.

Director: How do you make something your own?

Woman: Well, I make the scores I work on my own. I play them the way *I* would play them.

Director: So an executive plays the strategy the way he or she would play it. That makes it their own? But is there any other way to play it than to play it your way? I mean, when we play something we always play it our way.

Woman: No, I don't think you understand. Many people try to play the way someone else would play. It's difficult to play your own way. You have to find your way first. Finding your way is no easy thing.

Director: I take your point. But I wonder. Does an effective strategist take the executive's way into account when formulating the strategy?

Woman: That would be a good idea. It's like writing a score with the violinist in mind.

Director: Shall we take it further? Does the philosopher take the strategist's way into account when formulating the truth?

Woman: No, we shouldn't take it further. What does it mean to formulate the truth? That sounds outrageous, if you ask me.

Director: What if we only give them some of the truth, the truth that suits them best? Maybe that's a better way to put it?

Woman: Holding back truth? That doesn't sound good.

Director: But it might be more effective. Certain truths can get in the way of the best plans.

Woman: If you want to put plan above truth, be my guest. And if you want to put execution above plan, go right ahead. But I think it's a rotten way to go.

Director: So it's truth above all, strategy beneath, and execution at bottom?

Woman: That doesn't sound right either. Truth should be at bottom and...

Director: ...execution at top?

Woman: Something is wrong about our discussion of these things.

Director: Maybe we can combine all three. I mean, if we make truth our own, it's a part of us; if we make the strategy our own, likewise; and if we make the execution our own...

Woman: ...that's the perfect plan. It's the plan we'd be most comfortable with.

Director: But is comfort really what's most important here? Are we assuming making something our own makes it comfortable? What if our own gives us discomfort?

Woman: We're not comfortable with ourselves. Yes, that's a problem. Maybe we should get comfortable with ourselves before we try to make anything our own?

Director: What if there's no time? We're presented with a plan. We have to decide. What do we do?

Woman: I say we don't even try to make this plan our own. We execute it for what it is, assuming we have no choice.

Director: And if we execute enough plans like this, might our own will change?

Woman: I think there's a decent chance it will, assuming these are high quality plans.

Director: Why make that assumption? Even if not, it's likely our own will change. What we do changes us, no matter its quality.

Woman: Yes, but we want high quality so we can change for the best.

Director: How do you know low quality won't change us in a good way?

Woman: What do we mean by high and low quality?

Director: What would you like us to mean?

Woman: High quality has the greatest fidelity to truth. Low quality has a loose relationship to truth.

Director: So a high quality performance has the greatest fidelity to the score?

Woman: That's a fine way of looking at it.

Director: And a high quality judicial decision has the greatest fidelity to the Constitution.

Woman: Yes.

Director: But can the performer and judge do this while being uncomfortable? Haven't you ever played to a standing ovation while being uncomfortable?

Woman: I... have. But then again, the audience didn't really know the score.

DECISIONS

Director: Can the same be said about a judge and her or his performance in court? They were uncomfortable but came to a widely hailed decision.

Woman: Sure, that can happen. But I bet most judges stay within their comfort zone.

Director: No doubt. But some are brave and go without. Why do you think they do?

Woman: There are two reasons. One, they recognize the rightness of the interpretation of law. Two, popular pressure leads them that way.

Director: Well, I can imagine unpopular pressure leading that way, too. But I think you're right. Popular pressure certainly tells at times. But what's this about rightness of interpretation.

Woman: The simple interpretation is best. Some judges, and many lawyers, make convoluted arguments to support their cause. Arguments like that are never right.

Director: Some *people* make such arguments concerning themselves and their actions. Are they always wrong?

Woman: I think so, yes.

Director: What if they're comfortable with their labyrinthine reasoning?

Woman: Is anyone really comfortable with that?

Director: Oh, I think so. They're so familiar with their twists and turns they take comfort in them, sure. It helps them hide.

Woman: Hide from themselves, for one. They don't want a straight answer about what they're up to in life—both for themselves and others.

Director: So if they decide to do something questionable and say, 'Here are my many reasons for this,' they'll hope we fall asleep along the way.

Woman: Fall asleep, lose interest, go away. That's what they want. But do you know what we do when confronted with this? We cut to the chase.

Director: But let me guess. They consider this rude.

Woman: Absolutely, and they'll ask you to be patient. It takes a fight to get them to get to the point. And then things are ruined, because they're in a bad mood and not willing to talk.

Director: I know someone like this. Every story begins with the creation of the Earth and slowly leads its way, with very many tangents and asides, to the thing in question; and just when you think you'll get a straight answer, something always intervenes—usually because you've reached limit of tolerance for this.

Woman: You know it well. That's why we have judge based on what they do, not on what they say. And sometimes very innocent people are this way.

Director: Do you know why?

Woman: I don't. Do you have any ideas?

Director: I think it has to do with justice. The person believes that if only you knew *all* of the facts, you'd do justice them. And that's what they want most in all the world.

Woman: Don't you? Doesn't everyone? We all want justice done to us—we good people, anyway.

Director: Hmm. Justice is getting what we deserve? What do we deserve? Who gets to say?

Woman: Well, yes—that's a problem. Who decides? Judges, certainly—those who wear robes. But judges, too, in everyday life.

Director: Are they quick to judge, slow to judge—does it matter either way?

Woman: Each of us in our own case would like to know that the decision is made with all the facts. So slow to judge is best.

Director: Haven't you heard that justice must be swift?

Woman: Justice must be swift, not judgment.

Director: And yet justice is more important than judgment. Or is it?

Woman: Justice is the highest thing. We all, even the base, must judge.

Director: Why do we have to judge? Why not just decide? I can decide I don't like someone without judging them to be bad. Or are all those we don't like bad?

Woman: No, I'm not saying that. That would be grossly unfair. People can be different without being bad. Isn't that what philosophy says?

Director: I'm... not sure.

What Philosophy Says

Woman: You're not sure? What *does* philosophy say?

Director: Different philosophers have said different things about this. Did you think philosophy speaks with one voice?

Woman: The truth speaks with one voice. So I would expect philosophy to bring it all in line.

Director: But that's the thing. One of the greatest German philosophers of the nineteenth century said that truth is most when many truthful voices are heard. This means to view things from many different angles. The more angles, the more truth is seen.

Woman: So what does that mean? It takes a dozen philosophers to find truth enough to screw in a light bulb?

Director: Maybe. But that dozen could likely do many other things. Some philosophers are mechanically inclined; some philosophers are metaphysically inclined; some philosophers can speak to aesthetics; some philosophers can speak to a will to kill.

Woman: Soldier philosophers? I didn't know there was such a thing.

Director: Socrates served in the army. Machiavelli tried to reform Florentine arms.

Woman: I heard Socrates was known for a fabulous retreat. And if I'm not mistaken, Machiavelli never swung a sword in anger. Do you have any other examples?

Director: My point is that philosophers come in many sizes and shapes, and are good at different things.

Woman: So they're like everyone in that.

Director: Yes, but they have philosophy in common.

Woman: I've read some philosophy, you know. I can't say I've seen a common definition of what philosophy is.

Director: There is a definition. But it's very hard to arrive at it on your own.

Woman: Then share it with me.

Director: Better you come to it on your own. But I can give you a clue. It has to do with belief.

Woman: Then I know. Philosophy seeks true belief.

Director: Yes, that's certainly true. But I'm not sure it's in the sense you mean.

Woman: What sense do *you* mean?

Director: Philosophy seeks true believers and asks them why.

Woman: Why they believe?

Director: Yes, philosophy wants to know.

Woman: And when they explain it to you, you'll believe?

Director: If they can explain it with sufficient force? Maybe.

Woman: What force is sufficient for you?

Director: The force that takes away doubt.

Woman: And without doubt philosophy does what, act?

Director: Philosophy acts without a doubt.

Woman: Then philosophy is crippled by doubt.

Director: Philosophers must learn to overcome. We can doubt yet act. In fact, such action is like reconnaissance in force.

Woman: What does that mean?

Director: We seek to know the enemy force by probing and harassing them. How they react says much.

Woman: About where they're strong; about where they're weak? And what do you do? Attack the weakness you find?

Director: Of course.

Woman: And the strength?

Director: We attack them there, too; best when we've captured the higher ground.

Woman: Metaphorical higher ground?

Director: We're talking about beliefs. The battle is largely metaphorical.

Woman: How can it be direct?

Director: By making it direct.

FALSE BELIEF

Woman: So what are we talking about? Action against a false belief? What do we do? Supplant the false with true belief?

Director: What's the difference between true and false belief?

Woman: False belief harms; true belief helps.

Director: Helps what?

Woman: The person who believes. Belief can be a real source of strength.

Director: I have little doubt. And this strength is employed along the lines of the belief?

Woman: Naturally. So I wonder if philosophy should challenge the belief, or attempt to alter the lines—change the direction of the belief.

Director: That seems like a last resort—but not a bad step. How do we make a belief that leads to X lead to Y?

Woman: You tempt it with Z and hope it meets you halfway.

Director: And if it comes all the way over to Z?

Woman: We rejoice!

Director: But what is Z? Another kind of belief, true or false?

Woman: Z is the truth.

Director: And halfway to the truth is... what?

Woman: Better than further away.

Director: But don't you know that nothing lies better than lies that are close to truth? Maybe it's best to keep the lie at X, so people can see it for what it is.

Woman: You want X to leap to Z? Is that what philosophy does? Ask people to make a leap?

Director: There's no other way. All philosophers have had to make a leap.

Woman: Why?

Director: Because they recognize that the middle ground is bad.

Woman: It's uncomfortable.

Director: To put it mildly, yes. You're a philosopher or you're not. If you're not, stay at A. Don't attempt to be a B. And if you want in, make the leap to C.

Woman: Who is B in this world?

Director: Priests and priest-like characters, of which there are many in curious places. In fact, today there are more priest-like characters than there are priests.

Woman: And by A you mean alpha males and females and the like. But what do you mean by C?

Director: I just like the play of C and 'see'. Don't take any of this too seriously. They're just attempts to get near the point.

Woman: Why not go directly to the point?

Director: For the same reason you can't fly directly into the sun.

Woman: We'll go blind?

Director: Or burn right up.

Woman: Really, I think you philosophers take yourself too seriously. You imagine you have all sorts of power with your words. What do you say to that?

Director: My words only have power with those who are looking to be stimulated by words.

Woman: Who looks for that?

Director: Lovers of words.

Woman: That's a prerequisite of philosophy? You have to love words? Then why aren't poets philosophers? Why aren't lawyers? Why aren't authors?

Director: My words may have power with them. They don't transform them into philosophers. These people don't want to be philosophers. They want to be, for the most part, if they're successful— who they are.

Woman: Only the unsuccessful want to be philosophers?

Director: It's a very hard thing to say.

SUCCESS

Woman: You can say it to me. I won't judge. Is the reason you're a philosopher because you weren't otherwise successful?

Director: I'm successful in my job.

Woman: But do you really care about your job?

Director: Of course I care about my job. It's how I earn my living.

Woman: Yes, but you strike me as someone who could earn a living many other ways.

Director: Things aren't as open and free as you might think. My experience limits me to the sort of job I'm in. I'm not old, but I'm old enough that a change in career would be difficult.

Woman: Yes, but you can do difficult things.

Director: I have other difficult things I need to do.

Woman: Philosophy. You need your strength for that.

Director: Yes. Could I establish myself elsewhere? Yes, probably. But then I have no time for my true pursuit.

Woman: What do you do in this pursuit? Talk? Read? Write?

Director: Those are the things philosophers do. But you're missing an important thing. They also act.

Woman: And you're missing an important thing. They think.

Director: Thank you for reminding me. I've been so enjoying our talk I almost forgot.

Woman: That's what a successful conversation is to you? Something that makes you forget about thought? And here I was flattering myself that I was making you think, a little.

Director: You *have* made me think. But, odd as it may seem, some of our best thoughts we forget about right way. Later they make themselves felt.

Woman: Why aren't they successful in making us think right away?

Director: For one, it's hard to think extensively when engaged in conversation. For another, they seem innocent at first. It's only with time that their proportions are known.

Woman: Great proportion means serious thought?

Director: Small things take on great proportion *because* they promote serious thought.

Woman: What if these small things meet with no success? What if they are simply digested at once and go no further.

Director: What we digest becomes who we are, small or large. Small things have an advantage because they tend not to set off alarms.

Woman: So you engage in a philosophy of small things?

Director: Sometimes large; sometimes small. Today it's been a combination of things.

Woman: But are large things the serious things and small things the light?

Director: Are large things heavy? Not necessarily. We can deal lightly with large things. I think we've done some of that today. And we can be heavy when it comes to small things. This sort of thing happens every day. Think of all the heated arguments over little things.

Woman: Yes, but philosophers don't get heated.

Director: I think that's a prejudice. Philosophers can certainly get heated. In fact, I'd take their pulse to make sure they're alive if they never got heated. There's much to get heated about in this world.

Woman: You don't think philosophical success involves not getting worked up?

Director: Why shouldn't a philosopher get worked up? Is the philosopher so above everything that passion can't touch?

Woman: That statement's a little vague.

Director: Ah, you're right on the ball. It's certainly possible to be 'worked up' without being worked up. We call that an act. Yes, philosophers do this. But do they actually get worked up? I believe the answer is yes.

Woman: Yes, but then they lose their edge!

Director: Sometimes passion provides the greatest edge. Should philosophers be inhuman? Make no mistake. I think they need to be in command of themselves. But sometimes it's best to let go of the reins.

Woman: You have to *know* it's best to let go of the reigns.

Director: It's nice when you do. But sometimes you go with your gut, and a pretty good guess.

LETTING GO

Woman: I know a lot of people who are afraid to let go. They're wrapped very tight. They're afraid they'll unravel.

Director: They just have to ravel out the tangles once they've done. Not easy, of course. But pleasant if unravelling was fun.

Woman: So you admit we unravel when letting go.

Director: If we must be wrapped up, I think we need to be loose. It allows us to breathe. Besides, do we really need to be wrapped?

Woman: Should we walk around naked instead?

Director: No, but simple loose garb is best. We can get in and out of it with ease.

Woman: What are you really saying when it comes to letting go?

Director: I mean I don't have infinite patience—nor do I want to. At a certain point enough is enough. So I let go, and my temper comes through—my naked temper, yes. People for so long have been so afraid of this.

Woman: The lower walks of life let go like this all the time.

Director: Yes, but higher life isn't distinguished from lower life by patience or what have you. In fact, I would say higher life should have *less* patience than lower life. It's in need of it less.

Woman: How do you figure?

Director: Higher life is in command. It can afford to let loose now and then. Lower life, subject to higher life, must of necessity have more control—in order to protect itself from the high.

Woman: Then why does experience teach the opposite of what you say?

Director: Because people aren't aware of how things stand.

Woman: Oh, I think they're aware.

Director: Then it's a matter of history, custom, habit. Self-command somehow became a desired state for the upper classes a long time ago. I don't claim to know the genealogy of this. But I know it's there.

Woman: And why would the lower classes let go?

Director: There must be a mechanism that makes their rage impotent. So they are free to indulge in it with no real effect.

Woman: And philosophers?

Director: Holding tight protected them for a long stretch of time. But now they can afford to let go.

Woman: Protected them as if they were from the lower class?

Director: As if they were, and they were, untouchables.

Woman: What's so bad about philosophy?

Director: You can only ask that question because philosophers today are still all wrapped up. If they unwrapped themselves, if they let go...

Woman: ...they'd be like you? Are you really in the habit of letting go?

Director: I'm in the habit of self-control. But I don't always let habit win.

Woman: I'd like to see you let go.

Director: It isn't pretty.

Woman: Do you think I only care about the pretty? I guess you don't know me well enough yet. What would make you let go?

Director: For me, it's as I've said. My patience wears thin. I can only take so much nonsense before I let loose.

Woman: It doesn't matter the source?

Director: It doesn't matter the source.

Woman: I can see how that might get you in trouble. It might be your boss, a client, your wife....

Director: I'm not married. I have gotten into trouble with the other two, though.

Woman: Did you apologize?

Director: No.

Woman: On principle?

Director: No. We agreed to move on. And I made up for it in other ways.

Woman: By doing good work.

Director: By doing excellent work. If it weren't for that I don't think I'd survive. People wouldn't put up with me.

Woman: I think you're too hard on yourself.

Director: You haven't seen me at work.

Luck or Fate

Woman: Do you think the doctors told us the truth about the risks?

Director: Of the surgeries? Why wouldn't they? They want to prepare us for the worst, as well as insure against possible failure.

Woman: If we think the procedure is risky we won't blame them too much if they fail. Well, that's probably true. What are the odds we'd meet like this?

Director: Are you asking if our meeting is luck, or fate?

Woman: What's the difference? It just... is. Tell me the odds.

Director: Well, there are several billion people in the world....

Woman: No, don't tell me that. I'm just saying I think it's great luck.

Director: You don't believe in fate?

Woman: What's to believe? Fate either is or it isn't. My belief, or unbelief, won't change that one bit.

Director: So you're a fatalist about fate? How Russian of you.

Woman: You don't like the Russians?

Director: I'm not saying that. I'll tell you something. When I was boy, during the Cold War, I used to root for the Russians in the Olympics.

Woman: Why?

Director: Because they had something I'd never seen. A complete sense of serious purpose. It was as if they had nothing going for them but this.

Woman: And the American athletes lacked purpose? Then how did they ever win medals?

Director: They had purpose. But there was something *fatal* about the Russians. Or so my boyish sense told me. If they didn't win it was the end. Of course, I realize now that it wasn't that stark. But I'm persuaded there is something to this.

Woman: The Russians had fate while the Americans had luck. Not strictly speaking, no. But is that what you mean?

Director: It's hard to get at what I mean. Here are two examples that I think will shed light. An American won some event, I can't remember which. He positive beamed and danced on the podium. But then I saw a Russian take gold. He didn't even smile.

Woman: And you admired that?

Director: It struck me. There was something in the contrast. Something I couldn't understand.

Woman: It sounds like you still can't. But you preferred the one who didn't smile.

Director: Yes. It resonated with me.

Woman: I wouldn't say you're frivolous, but you don't seem all that serious to me. I mean, I know you can be serious. But I don't think you take it too far. Not even smiling over your win—that takes it too far. I think you, the boy, were fascinated. That's all.

Director: You're probably right. And maybe this wasn't a Russian phenomenon. Maybe there are people all over the world as serious as that.

Woman: What do you think they have in common?

Director: An overwhelming sense of fate.

Woman: Can we take fate lightly? I can't see how.

Director: A philosopher can.

Woman: His own fate?

Director: He's not sure if he knows it's his. At times he feels serious; at times he feels light.

Woman: How can you not be sure you know? Isn't knowing, knowledge, something you... know?

Director: I've been fooled before. That's why I have my doubts. Besides, if I do have a fate, my not knowing it will change... nothing.

NOTHING

Woman: If nothing is a noun, an actual *thing*, will your not knowing change it? You said it would *change* nothing.

Director: You're very funny. I'm glad you joke about my fate. I would say nothing can't be changed.

Woman: Because nothing *is*? Or are you saying all things can be changed?

Director: Only things *are*. Nothing, no thing, has no being. It can't be *is*. To your second point, I don't know if all things can be changed.

Woman: I still think you should be careful about your fate. Know it—and leave nothing alone.

Director: Which means to bother everything. Where is our conversation headed?

Woman: I don't know. But it's taking my mind off my friend. What happens if she dies? Is she... nothing? I know I'll be left with a void. That's nothingness, isn't it? A void?

Director: Voids are full of nothing, yes. And they can't be filled. What happens to your friend? I know, for us, she is no more.

Woman: I'm glad you didn't say something comforting, like she'll live on in the memories of my heart. Which is true. But I'm glad you didn't say it.

Director: You don't like being comforted.

Woman: I don't. I do like comfort, but not from another. I derive comfort from my own thoughts. Do you?

Director: Not always. Sometimes my thoughts are uncomfortable to think.

Woman: What do you do then? Change the way you think?

Director: That's a really good question. Yes, is the short answer. My thoughts in one area sometimes force—or persuade?—me to change my thoughts in another area.

Woman: Is there an area you'd never change? Some kind of core of thought? Or will your desire for comfort render suspect even that?

Director: Well, it's not exactly a desire for comfort.

Woman: What is it? A desire for truth? What do you want most? What? Are you reduced to silence?

Director: I'm trying to think. Give me a moment, please.

Woman: While you think, I'll think about what I want most. And you know what? It may well be comfort. Mental comfort. Bodily comfort. Comfort in my heart. I want it all. I want to be comfortable. And maybe that's true.

Director: All right—I have an answer for you. What I want most is dialogue.

Woman: What, you mean philosophical dialogue? Or are you talking about conversations in general?

Director: Conversations in general that have philosophical import. Like ours today.

Woman: How is that something anyone could possibly want most? I almost feel sorry for you.

Director: Dialogue stimulates both heart and mind. Is it easier to accept if I say what I want most is stimulation?

Woman: It is, in a funny sort of way. Funny because coffee stimulates. Do you want coffee more than anything in the world?

Director: Coffee stimulates, yes. I enjoy coffee quite a bit. It can help enliven conversation.

Woman: So can alcohol. Do you want that more than anything in the world? I know you don't. I just had to ask. But you're saying something other than stimulation, if you really think about it.

Director: What am I saying?

Woman: It's stimulation toward the end of dialogue, the consideration and exchange of ideas. That's what you want most. Am I right?

Director: You're right.

Woman: And if no living human is available for this, you turn to books. You strike me as a man who lives with books.

Director: It's true. I do.

Woman: Books are more alive to you than most human beings. Do you deny it?

Director: I don't.

Woman: Then my only question is this. Where will it get you in life?

LIFE

Director: People don't ask me that, you know.

Woman: They don't because you make lots of money. Everyone just assumes you're where you want to be, that you're doing well in life.

Director: And you don't?

Woman: I wonder if you ever get bored with your work. Boredom is the opposite of stimulation. And boredom is deadly. Oh, wait! I know what you do.

Director: What do I do?

Woman: You stir things up. If things get boring, you—for lack of a better word—cause trouble.

Director: What kind of trouble do you think I cause?

Woman: You find a loose end somewhere, some simple contradiction in thought—and you call it out. It doesn't matter if it's a subordinate, a peer, or your boss. You call it out.

Director: Then what?

Woman: You see where it goes. You're ready for anything, I suppose. A true philosopher.

Director: You're the first person I've come across who sees a philosopher for what he is.

Woman: Yes, yes—a man ready for anything. Anything! Do you know what that means?

Director: I have some idea.

Woman: That puts you at risk. That readiness, it gives off a scent that predators can smell a mile away. People will attack you for this—because you seem ready.

Director: I thought it might scare them off.

Woman: No. They will always mistake your readiness for having a chip on your shoulder. And they will seek to knock it off.

Director: And when they realize there's nothing to knock off?

Woman: They'll attack you personally. The logic of this is clear.

Director: Spell it out for me.

Woman: People like this don't like to be mistaken, as they were about the chip. And your refusal to retaliate seems like an affront. Baffled, they lash out. And you, you lash right back.

Director: Not quite. I don't lash; I subvert.

Woman: I knew it! You're a subversive! But you only subvert those who attack. But you know full well that your bearing will egg them on. In a way, you set the whole thing up.

Director: Why would I do that?

Woman: Because it stimulates you! I've figured you out.

Director: I guess you have.

Woman: But I find it a little hard to believe.

Director: What's so hard?

Woman: It's stimulation for stimulation's sake.

Director: Well, it does help with my thinking.

Woman: But then it's just thinking for thinking's sake.

Director: Is everything just for everything's sake?

Woman: In the end, it is.

Director: Then why does any of it matter? Everything we do in life is for everything we do. The point of anything is the point. Does that make sense?

Woman: I know exactly what you mean. It's liberating, in a way.

Director: Yes, it is. It makes you ready for anything.

Woman: Do you think *I* could be ready for anything? I who love comfort?

Director: It's possible to find comfort in a ready stance. But oftentimes what you encounter will not make you comfortable. Stimulated, maybe. But uncomfortable, yes.

Woman: I never thought about stimulated discomfort before. I'm not sure I like the idea.

Director: It's how philosophers stay alive.

IDEAS

Woman: The idea itself keeps you alive? The idea of stimulated discomfort?

Director: The ability to think uncomfortable thoughts keeps philosophers alive. I should have been more clear.

Woman: Yes, you really should have been more clear. But what's so great about uncomfortable thoughts?

Director: These thoughts, if we accept them, can help us grow. And no, it's not growth for the sake of growth, as in this being our great purpose.

Woman: But if you keep growing this way, won't you be stuffed full of ideas?

Director: Growth can amount to a narrowing of thought.

Woman: That's interesting, and counter intuitive. Give me an example.

Director: It's not very hard to understand. Suppose we believe ten petty ideas. Along comes a challenge that really makes us think. We learn one big idea, and jettison the rest. We've grown, but narrowed the scope of our thought from ten to one.

Woman: I think you're cheating in that example. The one idea has greater scope than the ten. Your thought hasn't narrowed. It's simplified, yes. But it's larger, of broader range, than before.

Director: It's not a point I care to argue. But ideas really are funny things. In a way, everything is an idea. Everything we can perceive enters the mind as an idea.

Woman: That's a prejudice of the philosophers. A rock is not an idea. A rock is a rock. Now, you might have ideas about what to do with the rock. But that's a different thing.

Director: I'm not sure I've ever been refuted that well.

Woman: I spend a lot of time alone with my violin. That gives me time to think.

Director: If only that violin could speak. But wait! It does, of course, speak! Better—it sings! But who can expound the ideas it voices?

Woman: I can, of course. I can articulate musical ideas. These ideas are emotions. Do philosophers care about emotions?

Director: They certainly do. They want to know what they mean.

Woman: Do you know what anger means?

Director: I have a few ideas. But it would take me several hours to spell it all out.

Woman: Maybe another time. Anger in music is violent, just like it is in people.

Director: That's not too hard to understand. And lightheartedness, is it light and sweet?

Woman: You'll be a psychologist of music in no time at this pace. It's so simple that anyone can be one.

Director: Then why don't you grow bored?

Woman: Because the basic ideas of music are like the primary colors. We don't get bored of color because the primaries are three.

Director: Wouldn't it be something if all the thought in the world boiled down to just three things?

Woman: It would be something. What three might they be? Or is that too speculative for a man of knowledge like you?

Director: Believe it or not, I have an imagination. The three might be latitude, longitude, and elevation.

Woman: What! That's stupid. Try again.

Director: Pleasure, pain, emptiness.

Woman: That's more interesting. I suppose you'll want me to try, as well. Alright. Sight, sound, taste, touch, smell.

Director: That's five.

Woman: That's my allowance for not being a philosopher. Try again.

Director: I just realized. An idea contains its opposite. So when I said pleasure, pain, emptiness—I only used two ideas. So it will be pleasure/pain, emptiness/fullness, and....

Woman: What's the matter? Did you run out of steam?

Director: Emptiness and fullness might collapse into pleasure and pain. And I don't want to say everything boils down to pleasure and pain.

Woman: Then you're going to have to think up some good ideas. But what's wrong with saying everything boils down to pleasure and pain? Isn't that my philosophy, if comfort is what I really want? Comfort is a pleasure; discomfort is a pain. Am I so bad?

BAD

Director: I don't think you're bad at all. Maybe a little evil, but definitely not bad.

Woman: Evil? Why, because I took a bite of the apple and liked the taste? I haven't seen you smile quite that way before.

Director: Everyone takes knowledge for granted today. Knowledge, we say, is good. But that's the easy knowledge, gotten with a good conscience. There are other types of knowledge.

Woman: Criminal knowledge. How it feels to steal. How it feels to kill. And yet knowledge, we say, is good. Well, it isn't always good. There's good knowledge and bad knowledge.

Director: Which did you mean in taking the bite?

Woman: I was bluffing, as you probably know. I don't have any unlawful knowledge.

Director: But music can portray how that knowledge feels. Right?

Woman: Definitely. I should play at a prison some time and talk with the prisoners afterwards, to see what they think. In fact, that's what I think an adventurous composer should do. Play a rough draft of his or her piece, then shape it from the reaction. That way they can get it right.

Director: Yes, but what if what sounds true to a convict sounds false to everyone else? What if it just sounds bad?

Woman: But it sounds good to the criminal. Hmm. I hadn't thought of that. And what if the only way for it to sound good is for everyone else to gain criminal knowledge? Then they'd know it's true.

Director: Such musical dilemmas. The problem is greater than that, too. There are things that are frowned upon, not illegal. That means music will have a similar problem here, as well.

Woman: But it's not the problem of music alone. Philosophy must have trouble here, too.

Director: Certainly. Something that seems unintelligible to most might seem perfectly intelligible to someone who wasn't afraid of frowns.

Woman: Afraid of frowns. It sounds so sad and yet it's very true. We are afraid of frowns. Frowns are uncomfortable.

Director: It takes some practice but you can get used to them.

Woman: But why would you want to? Frowns mean you're bad. Frowns are very hard to overcome.

Director: Overcoming stimulates.

Woman: And that's reason enough for you? Reason enough to be a bad boy?

Director: Our early experience shapes us here.

Woman: No doubt. Most of us never get beyond that shape. What shape is philosophy? What shape are you?

Director: As you see.

Woman: I'd hate to see you frown. I'm not sure I could take that much discomfort. But somehow I think you wouldn't terribly mind if I were to frown at you!

Director: I would depend on the reason. If I were somehow in the wrong, it would bother me. But if you were in the wrong, the frown wouldn't mean all that much.

Woman: What if you weren't sure who was right or wrong?

Director: The frown would stimulate me to think.

Woman: You make a loss into a win. I like that character trait. I wish I had it. Usually losses just get me down. They make me feel bad. I like to feel good. Maybe that's why I'm first chair. I'm very, very good. Do you like to feel good?

Director: Feel good as in have the approval of one who would judge? Approval is overrated.

Woman: Well, I'm one who rates it highly. I'd die if I got a bad review. Why am I so afraid?

Director: Maybe you're too comfortable? Too much comfort makes us afraid. Too much comfort is bad.

Woman: Isn't that strange. Comfort makes us afraid. Afraid we'll lose the comfort. But when we lose the comfort it's nothing but... discomfort. It's so very simple. So your big philosophical idea is to get me comfortable with discomfort.

Director: I think the idea is properly—yours.

BELONGING

Woman: Do you remember when you were a kid and someone would come up with an idea and someone else would *steal* the idea? 'Hey! That was *my* idea!' That poor kid who said that probably went on to become an intellectual property lawyer.

Director: My favorite is when the other person comes up with the idea independently and the kid still cries out, 'It's my idea!"

Woman: How do we own ideas? I'm not talking about patents. I'm talking about basic ideas. Philosophical ideas.

Director: We make them our own. But we can't stop others from making them their own.

Woman: They belong to whomever makes them their own. Yes, that makes sense.

Director: But I'm not sure I'd call them 'philosophical ideas'.

Woman: Why not? What would you call them? Aphilosophical ideas?

Director: To the extent people believe in them, yes.

Woman: What's that supposed to mean? Philosophers don't believe in their ideas? That's nonsense. No one could spend as much time on ideas as philosophers do and *not* believe in them. What would be the point? Philosophy would be a colossal waste of time.

Director: And maybe it is. But I am persuaded it's not.

Woman: What persuades you? But first, tell me if you believe?

Director: In my ideas? Ideas aren't knowledge.

Woman: Let me think about that. Aren't they?

Director: Ideas usually need to be acted upon before you can really know what they are.

Woman: You mean whether they're good or bad.

Director: Yes, something like that.

Woman: So you don't believe in the Platonic ideas.

Director: No, I don't.

Woman: Did Plato?

Director: I'm inclined to think he didn't.

Woman: Then why would he preach them?

Director: He didn't preach. He had characters in books talk about them.

Woman: Oh, that's nonsense. Everyone knows he believed in those ideas.

Director: I doubt what everyone knows. Usually the people who *know* haven't read the books. But why did you ask the question?

Woman: About Plato? I don't know. The question was in the air. I just reeled it in. But even if he didn't believe in those ideas, he belonged with them.

Director: That's an interesting statement. I don't think I ever would have put it that way.

Woman: Does that make me a philosopher?

Director: It makes you something, that's for sure. Not to belong *to*, but to belong *with*—as in among? Like a tree in a forest?

Woman: No, like a woodsman a forest. But I don't like that image because I don't want him to chop down the trees. Think of it like a tree-hugger in a forest.

Director: Plato hugs the ideas. That's funny. And he makes them his own. And for millennia others followed suit.

Woman: Do you want people to follow you?

Director: I don't think they could.

Woman: Why, are you so positively able and tough?

Director: No, I just mean my way is my way alone.

Woman: The lonely philosopher. Does each of us have our own way?

Director: No. Most people aren't positively able and resilient enough to have their own way.

Woman: Ha! That's anti-democratic, you know.

Director: Is it? I just know it's true.

ANTI

Woman: There are certain antis you just can't be. Anti-democratic is one. Anti-family is another.

Director: That's it? Are those the big two? Are you sensing I'm somehow anti-family?

Woman: No, don't be ridiculous. It's that our freedom of expression has some serious limits. Sure you can say anything—but then you pay.

Director: What price do I pay for saying not everyone can have their own way?

Woman: With me? No price. But try saying that in public. Try writing a book that says most people are pathetic and weak. I don't think it would go over that well. The gist of all self-help books, for instance, is that anyone can do it. And self-health books sell.

Director: What if a book didn't have to *sell?* Wouldn't there be great freedom in that? Couldn't you say whatever you want?

Woman: No, there are still limits and prices to be paid. Even if you didn't have to worry about money, I think you'd still self-censor—out of fear.

Director: Prudence?

Woman: Yes, prudence. You need to be prudent when you write. But if you're *too* prudent, you fail to make your point.

Director: I see. So you have to walk the line. I wonder how comfortable it is on the line.

Woman: Probably not very. It's not very comfortable living in fear.

Director: But what are we saying? There have been philosopher-writers who have set down very provocative thoughts. If they weren't comfortable with it, why would they do it?

Woman: They were daring.

Director: That's it?

Woman: That's it.

Director: I like to put it this way. They were more generous with their thoughts than prudent.

Woman: Generous. Ha, ha. I like that, too. But look at the price many of them paid for their generosity. Some were arrested. Some were banished. Some were put to death. And some simply went mad. The last one interests me most.

Director: People use the madness as an argument against the thought.

Woman: Yes, and it's really not fair. The philosophers' beautiful, unpopular thought put them at odds with the world. And the pressure from *that* drove them mad.

Director: Yes, that seems likely. Though I do think it's something of a chicken and egg question.

Woman: What, madness made them have the beautiful thoughts? Or madness caused them to dare the crowd to punish them?

Director: I don't know. I think it's complicated.

Woman: But you're a philosopher! You should know.

Director: Maybe I don't know myself as well as you might think.

Woman: Isn't that the first imperative of philosophers? *Know thyself?*

Director: I think the first imperative is to resist the crowd.

Woman: So you're anti-crowd. Even if you come to a concert of mine? You'd be part of the crowd. Or don't you think my kind of music is given to crowds? Maybe it's more of a gathering?

Director: If it's a crowd, it's a well behaved crowd. Maybe it *is* a gathering—certainly as opposed to a mob.

Woman: When was the last time you saw a mob?

Director: I've only seen a few. One, after our team won the football championship. Another when I was in the service.

Woman: What was the second one like?

Director: I was in a helicopter over it all for most of it. It was ugly. People were getting hurt.

Woman: Did anyone die?

Director: Yes.

Woman: Anyone you knew?

Director: Yes.

APOLOGIES

Woman: I'm so sorry.

Director: Don't be. You didn't stir up the mob. You didn't kill my friend.

Woman: Did you see him die?

Director: I did.

Woman: Were you... overcome with grief?

Director: I focused on killing those who killed him. I suppose that took my mind off the grief.

Woman: Were you... successful?

Director: I was.

Woman: How do you feel about it all now?

Director: Apparently not too, too bad—because I can talk about it with you.

Woman: Does your... conscience ever bother you? I'm sorry. I don't mean to pry. I just would really like to know.

Director: Mostly my conscience says an eye for an eye, a tooth for a tooth is good. I'm pretty comfortable with that.

Woman: But not entirely. I think I can understand, as much as someone can understand something like this. But, enough. Symphony listeners are not a dangerous mob.

Director: Not directly, at least.

Woman: What do you mean? How so? How are they dangerous? Do you think it's because they're rich, and the rich are dangers to the poor? Not everyone who attends is rich.

Director: No, it's not a matter of money. It's a matter of taste. That's what happens in a democracy.

Woman: What do you mean?

Director: We're all supposed to be equal. So the rich are uncomfortable concerning the poor. They want to distinguish themselves from them. They rely on taste.

Woman: I think of someone saying, 'I have expensive tastes.'

Director: Yes, that someone usually thinks the tastes distinguish them from the rest.

Woman: How *should* we distinguish ourselves from the rest?

Director: Through our thought. A truly free thinker is unique.

Woman: How do we know if we're truly unique?

Director: The pressure from the crowd grows immense.

Woman: So what can we do?

Director: Not take it all that seriously.

Woman: Ha! Being all alone in the crowd, under tremendous pressure— and making light of it? That's no small trick!

Director: It's not a trick. It's a stance—one you can grow more and more comfortable in.

Woman: So you're saying that the unique don't care.

Director: Concerning many things, yes. They just don't care.

Woman: But prudence keeps them honest.

Director: I thought you would have said prudence keeps them *dishonest*— pretending that they care. Because, after all, the crowd wants to know you care about them—even if only as a threat.

Woman: What happens when you don't?

Director: The crowd knows. Let me give you an example. During the foot-ball mob, I was walking a friend to the train. He was outraged at the mob, and let his outrage show. The mob picked up on this. Someone threw a beer bottle at his head. Another came up and gave him a shove and said crass things. They *sensed* he wasn't with them. He couldn't care less about football. Somehow they knew.

Woman: They always know. I feel sorry for your friend.

Director: Oh, don't feel sorry. He is defiant by nature. I was more worried for him than he was worried for himself.

Woman: But he put you at risk, as well.

Director: That he did. But that wasn't on his mind.

Dangerous

Woman: That's a dangerous friend to have.

Director: He was a good friend, a very good friend—but dangerous, too. Or should I say—*and* dangerous, too?

Woman: Say whatever you like. I don't have dangerous friends. I have casual friends. Pleasant friends.

Director: If that's what you're comfortable with, then that's fine.

Woman: Are you comfortable with dangerous friends?

Director: For a time, until the danger comes too near.

Woman: What do you do? Abandon your friend?

Director: No. I tell them that they're putting us at serious risk. And friends don't do that to friends.

Woman: So you put them on notice. And then what? You have to break things off if they don't listen.

Director: I make it uncomfortable for them.

Woman: You're trying to make *them* break things off? That seems a little underhanded, if you ask me.

Director: Why? I'm giving them a chance to change risky behavior.

Woman: Yes, but you suggested you knew they were dangerous going into things. You play for a while and then you're done.

Director: You make me sound so bad. What if I told you I don't *play* for a while, I *try* for a while—try to make them see the risks they're taking are no good? If that kind of reasoning doesn't work, I show them the risks to me.

Woman: You hope they'll be ashamed at putting you at risk?

Director: Not much shame. Maybe a sense of duty? Sometimes people won't act for their own sake, but they will for someone else.

Woman: Maybe. But what's in this sort of friendship for you? A taste of excitement, adventure? Be honest. You like the risk.

Director: I like risk when it's necessary for a certain reward. I don't like senseless risk. Scowling at a mob in heat, when in the midst of it, is risky—and has no real reward.

Woman: Real? Do you think it has imaginary reward? In the mind of your friend? It must, mustn't it?

Director: I don't think he was thinking about any reward. He disapproved. I disapproved. But he wanted them to *know* he disapproved. I saw no good in that.

Woman: What do you think was the difference between you two?

Director: He had contempt for the mob. The mob was beneath him, and he wanted that to be clear.

Woman: What kind of mob was this? A dozen people?

Director: Thousands.

Woman: Oh. He was foolish, wasn't he?

Director: Very. Contempt in such circumstances is very indulgent. Not only did he not give any thought to his own safety, he gave none to mine.

Woman: Why would someone act this way?

Director: Because he has a very high opinion of himself. Now, I had a very high opinion of him. But his own was higher still—too high.

Woman: The man who quelled the mob through pure force of personality and will.

Director: Yes. And do you know what's crazy? He was comfortable in that imagined role.

Woman: Nothing he could do or say could quell that mob. He really couldn't see it?

Director: No, I think he could see it. I think he didn't care.

GOOD AND BAD

Woman: What I find amazing is that it was probably more comfortable for him to face the mob than to keep quiet and hurry away. There's something good in that. Something brave.

Director: I agree. But good in the wrong places is often bad.

Woman: What prevents good from knowing where it should be?

Director: Fixed ideas. My friend thought of himself as the righter of wrongs. The mob was wrong; he was going to straighten it out.

Woman: That's interesting. I always thought of fixed ideas as something outside yourself, a belief about the way the world is.

Director: Yes, but the worst fixed ideas concern ourselves.

Woman: Do you have the fixed idea that you're a philosopher?

Director: No, I question that idea all the time. What is a philosopher? What am I? It has to be both, both questions. My friend could have asked, 'What is a high and mighty man? What am I?' And maybe he did. Maybe he asked himself all the time.

Woman: But when push came to shove he knew.

Director: When push came to shove I'm inclined to say he had a fixed idea, something he believed with his whole being.

Woman: Why didn't he know?

Director: Because when you know, you talk about things a certain way. When you believe, you have another way about you.

Woman: A way about you. That's the difference between good or bad? A certain way?

Director: What can I say? It's more complicated than that, but that's the gist.

Woman: Do I believe or do I know?

Director: About yourself? I think you have a pretty good idea.

Woman: A pretty good idea! Ha! Then why can't I say with confidence what I am?

Director: Because that's usually what true believers do.

Woman: Your friend was that way? He spoke of himself?

Director: Oh, yes—he certainly did speak.

Woman: And you can't speak that way.

Director: I *can* speak that way—but I don't.

Woman: What would allow you speak that way?

Director: To fix an idea about myself in my head. It's not that hard to do. After a while it gets easier. You build up momentum.

Woman: And momentum this way is bad. But then what's good?

Director: Whatever fights mental inertia. Fixed ideas are the pillars of inertia.

Woman: And would you be Samson and push out the pillars and bring the temple down upon you?

Director: And kill all my enemies? Tempting, but no.

Woman: Not even if you were very old?

Director: One foot in the grave? That's a different calculus.

Woman: Ha! I think you'd do it. What's that French saying Dostoevsky likes to cite? 'Après moi, le déluge.' 'I don't care what happens after I'm gone.'

Director: That's the saying, but it doesn't quite fit. After my heroic act things should improve, no? I mean, if I bring down the temple of inertia....

Woman: Everything would be lively, true. I'm not sure what made me think of that saying.

149

Director: Maybe you were thinking of the alternate, literal sense. 'After me, the flood.' A flood of mental activity once inertia is gone.

Woman: Sure, that must have been it.

Director: Why do you smile at me so?

Woman: Because you offered me a generous interpretation.

Director: Don't you think interpretation should be generous?

Woman: I think good interpretation should strive to make clear the meaning intended by the one who spoke.

Director: But why do that if there's a better meaning to be found? Why not aim to find the best? Are you so anchored to your love for the truth of intent that you'd turn down something better?

Intent

Woman: My love for the truth of intent? Aren't you being a little presumptuous here? I never said I love the truth of intent, whatever that means.

Director: I'm sorry. I made a leap. Do you believe intent matters?

Woman: It does in the law—criminal intent. *Mens rea*, they call it. But that doesn't apply to every crime. Some crimes involve no intent at all.

Director: Well, bad books written with no intent to be bad are certainly bad—so I agree.

Woman: You agree? Ha! What about good books written with no intent to be good?

Director: What, they're good on accident? I'd celebrate the good! And make it clear, gently, to the author—that I know he or she didn't know what they were about.

Woman: Why bother to make that clear?

Director: So there's a chance that the next book will be good, too. And not just because of luck. Also, I'm not one to promote hubris. It's good to keep an author honest. When there's a lucky strike, not too many do.

Woman: Well, you'll make an honest woman of me yet. But I do think intent is important. It shows the difference between those who are trying and those who are just cruising in their comfort zone.

Director: I like to cruise in my comfort zone. Don't you?

Woman: Everyone does. But there are times when we need to turn off cruise control and try.

Director: No doubt. When is it such a time?

Woman: We can just... tell. Something in us says it's time. Something in our heart.

Director: Is our mind in comfort but our heart full of unrest? Or does the heart trouble the mind?

Woman: The heart troubles the mind. In fact, I think the intent of the heart wants to break through.

Director: Break through *what* in the mind?

Woman: Inertia. When we're on cruise control, that's as much inertia as standing still. I know my physics. We have to resist the urge to stay unchanged.

Director: How often do we change? Or that's what the heart tells us.

Woman: Yes, the heart tells us when we need to change. And that change can be so painful you wouldn't believe it. But it's necessary.

Director: What happens if we don't change?

Woman: We die inside. The heart shrivels and dies. And then there's no coming back. We can fight the need to change. We can dig in with all our might. But it's no good.

Director: How do we know which way to change?

Woman: You have to try something. And then you'll know it when you see it. You'll know the way. But, again, this can be very painful. Painful like you wouldn't believe. But it must be done.

Director: Are you thinking of relationships?

Woman: I am. But isn't all of life one great big relationship with everyone we meet? The biggest change is within, with how you deal with others. And this is very scary stuff.

Director: Tell me, Woman. Can we know the heart's intent? Does the heart even have an intent?

Woman: The heart wants us to thrive—whatever that means, and I know it's problematic.

Director: What's the problem with thriving? I think everyone should.

Woman: Sometimes, in order to thrive, you must do things others won't like.

Director: Ah. Problematic. So why not just do them? Unproblematic.

Woman: It's not so simple. Relationships can get very complex, tangled. We can't untangle ourselves with ease.

Director: Cut the knot.

Woman: Yes, you like that phrase I see.

CONSEQUENCES

Director: What's the worst that can happen? Someone will be mad at you?

Woman: It's more a matter of alienating your family and friends.

Director: You'll make them alien? Maybe you'll reveal they're alien. You can't make people other than they are.

Woman: I'm the one who's alien.

Director: So you want to hide yourself to protect your truth? Maybe that's why your relationships are tangled. You're not being yourself.

Woman: Are you yourself?

Director: Sometimes it's not easy to be yourself. And when you are, there are consequences. I'm someone who accepts the consequences.

Woman: You alienate your family and friends.

Director: I won't deny that happens from time to time. But usually I alienate others—people I'm meeting for the first time, people at work, people in general whenever I must deal with them.

Woman: How can you cope with so much alienation? I don't know that I could.

Director: For every nine I alienate, let's say, there's one who appreciates me for me. That's a fine trade, if you ask me.

Woman: But don't those nine all turn on you?

Director: What can they do? Give me a hard time? That's one of the consequences I accept. I'm willing to work through the hard. Too many are lazy and cowardly here.

Woman: I am lazy and cowardly here. It just seems so overwhelming. I don't know how you do it.

Director: So you believe me that I do it? Why?

Woman: I don't know. There's something honest in how we're talking today. I'm inclined to believe what you say.

Director: Yes, but now I must say. You don't strike me as lazy and cowardly at all.

Woman: That's because you don't know me very well. I'm afraid of people making things hard for me. I get along with most everyone *because* I'm afraid.

Director: Well, you're not alone in this. I don't recommend it. But it will take a re-architecting of your personality.

Woman: Ha! That's pretty blunt. How do you re-architect a personality?

Director: One difficult step at a time.

Woman: How long does it take?

Director: A good twenty-five years.

Woman: Stop. Are you serious? You are serious! How would you know?

Director: I've been working mine for a while. I'm a constant work in progress.

Woman: Oh, then it doesn't sound so scary. We're all constant works in progress—those of us that work, anyway. Some people are nothing in progress.

Director: I'd up it and say *many* are nothing in progress.

Woman: Are you a believer in progress? In general, not just in yourself.

Director: What would progress in general mean? What would progress? Civilization? Humanity? The world?

Woman: Any of those will do. But let's focus on humanity. Progress?

Director: I'm not inclined to believe it. Humanity is what humanity is. After all, humanity is an idea. Ideas can evolve, I suppose—but it's not necessarily progress when they do.

Woman: What does humanity mean to you? What's your idea of the idea?

Director: I don't really have one.

Woman: What? How can you not? You have one even if you think you don't. It's not possible to *live* without an idea of humanity.

Director: Either it's possible or I'm dead. But I think it's possible. I have an interest in so thinking. I like to be numbered among the living. But what do you really think the consequences are of not having any idea concerning humanity?

Woman: You'll either make yourself incredibly open minded—or you'll make yourself into a terrible monster.

MONSTERS 2

Director: Why a monster?

Woman: The idea of humanity is a bond that unites us. Monsters don't unite with others.

Director: And that makes them... monstrous? What's so good about uniting?

Woman: It gives a sense of belonging—and it prevents you from doing others harm.

Director: When you belong you feel comfortable, right?

Woman: Of course. And I know what you're going to say. Comfort prevents us from doing harm. Well, if it's true, it's a wonderful thing.

Director: I'll say. To be good you just have to be comfortable. So monsters are, essentially, uncomfortable.

Woman: But that's ridiculous to say. Monsters might be very comfortable indeed in all the harm they work. In fact, I think some of the most comfortable are the most monstrous!

Director: So where does that leave us?

Woman: We can't judge good or bad from comfort alone.

Director: We two are regular philosophers. Who else could make such a profound moral discovery?

Woman: What do you really think makes for a monster?

Director: Have you ever had your wisdom teeth pulled?

Woman: No, I haven't. Have you?

Director: Yes. It's not too painful. But if you don't do it, and they're impacted, there can be constant trouble—pain, infection, and other difficulties.

Woman: Including bad breath, I've heard.

Director: That's what I hear. So what makes for a monster? Some who has impacted ideas.

Woman: The ideas need to be pulled?

Director: Yes. And an impacted idea is much, much worse than an impacted tooth. The pain and mental infection that comes from such an idea drives a person to become monstrous.

Woman: So a philosopher must remove the idea.

Director: It doesn't always take a philosopher. But in bad cases I recommend it.

Woman: Have you removed an impacted idea? And while we're at it, tell me what it means for an idea to be impacted.

Director: Ideas are impacted when they get stuck, to put it simply. They can't go anywhere. Have I done this? Have I remove a stuck idea? I've worked with someone to remove the idea themselves. But I've never pulled one out myself.

Woman: Not even for yourself?

Director: Oh, of course for myself! Ideas have a tendency to want to become stuck, fixed. They're funny that way. I've been fortunate in that I've been able to remove my ideas before they become too fixed.

Woman: But what does that mean? You're always removing ideas?

Director: Most ideas are like weeds. You need to pull them up by the roots. But every now and then you get a beautiful plant or even a tree. And you nourish them. But I really think that's enough with the metaphor now.

Woman: That's fine. But just one more thing. The soul of a monster is like wild land— and the soul of a *what* is like cultivated land?

Director: It's hard to cultivate all our soul, but anyone can try. Here I think it's the effort that counts.

Woman: I think philosophers make beautiful gardens of their souls. You're just too modest to say.

Director: I think *you* make a garden of your soul. I've seen some beauty in you.

Woman: Some? You've seen *some* beauty in me?

Director: You're right to tease. I'm glad you're not offended by the *some*.

SOME

Woman: I take no offense because I'm a work in progress. I see some beauty in you, too. I think you have more experience gardening than I do. When did you start?

Director: I started preparing the soil when I was very young, as far back as I can remember. I was always pulling up weeds. But sometimes I pulled up healthy ideas.

Woman: How do you know they were healthy?

Director: I learned later from others. I offered to help them rip them up, and they said, 'No, this will make a fine tree one day.' Well, one day came and I saw.

Woman: You're talking about stretches of years.

Director: Some knowledge takes a long time, if you're learning from scratch. But one time knowledge came quickly. I wanted to rip up a weed, and someone said no—and they took me to a nursery, where I saw this 'weed' as a cherished growth. Live and learn.

Woman: I once hired someone to weed my garden, literally, and he ripped up half of the flowers.

Director: A rookie philosopher mistake. That's too bad. Did you pay him?

Woman: I'm embarrassed to admit it, but I did. Now I do all the weeding myself.

Director: I admit, I find it hard to know every flower from every weed. Sometimes I make mistakes.

Woman: You weed your own garden?

Director: Sorry, I was talking in the metaphor again.

Woman: Some metaphors are helpful.

Director: Yes, and some metaphors are fixed ideas. They cripple our ability to think.

Woman: Some so crippled are comfortable, no?

Director: Until things change and they find they can't adjust.

Woman: And then it's too late.

Director: For some, certainly. Others who are young enough in spirit can find ways to adapt. Those are the ones I want to help.

Woman: As a philosopher.

Director: Yes. As a human being.

Woman: What if they're not comfortable being helped?

Director: This kind of help is never comfortable.

Woman: It's like going to the dentist for the mind?

Director: I suppose I asked for that comparison myself. Yes, it's sort of like that.

Woman: So while you know it will be unpleasant, you know it's good for you. But how do you know?

Director: Some feel relief almost right away. They know it's good.

Woman: And others?

Director: That can be a long, painful work in progress.

Woman: Sort of like physical therapy?

Director: Yes, I think that's an apt comparison.

Woman: People in physical therapy have to take it on trust that things will get better. Is that how it is with you as a philosopher?

Director: It's a little different. I suggest some things then leave them to work it out themselves.

Woman: Why not stay with them?

Director: Because we're talking about the mind. And the mind is related to the heart. Those two things need to be worked on alone. The presence of another only distracts.

Woman: But when they've made some progress, don't they come back and show you?

Director: Often times, yes. And it's very nice to see. But I'll tell you. Some come back and they've gotten worse.

Woman: They didn't try?

Director: No, they tried. But they did themselves more harm than good. And so we talk and I show them some things and off they go alone again.

Woman: What's the most you've ever seen someone come back before they improved?

Director: More than I care to say.

LIMIT

Woman: Isn't there a limit to what you can take?

Director: If they're really trying, and they don't lash out at me, I'll keep trying, too.

Woman: You're better than I am. I don't think I could put up with that. Why do you?

Director: I love philosophical conversations, conversations where both sides are trying. I just can't turn one down. Besides, I admire those who try and fail yet try again.

Woman: Some never succeed?

Director: Yes, but then we have to ask what is success. Is it having a perfectly beautiful mind? There's no such thing. Every philosopher must try, and continue to try.

Woman: Yes, but you love to try.

Director: I do. And I'm hoping the one who fails will learn to love it, too.

Woman: Do you fail?

Director: Oh, all the time. I fail in this; I fail in that.

Woman: But you seem like a successful person to me.

Director: That's because I don't brag about the failures. I keep them in my workshop, which is closed to the public.

Woman: The public, sure. But what about friends? Don't you ever let them in?

Director: I have an anteroom to the shop. I bring friends there. That's where I draw the line. When I work on my heart and mind, it's work I do alone.

Woman: But you bring out the successes?

Director: I certainly do. And my friends are the first to know.

Woman: I'm glad. But now I wonder what we're even talking about!

Director: We're talking about limits. Limits to what we can take; limits to what we achieve; limits to what we share.

Woman: I thought philosophy knows no limits.

Director: In some ways, philosophy is the most limit bounded thing of all.

Woman: Why would that be?

Director: Philosophy can't be open to everything at once. It would be overwhelmed. So it must set limits. Limits allow philosophy to succeed.

Woman: Can you say more?

Director: Think of it this way. You want to overhaul your heart and mind because you know they're not right. Do you demolish everything at once in order to build everywhere at once?

Woman: Of course not. That would land you in a mental institution.

Director: Yes, exactly. This happens, you know. Some people try to make up for lost time and try to do everything at once—and they go mad. We have to work on one thing at a time. And we have to be patient. Patience is vital here.

Woman: So it's one idea at a time?

Director: One idea at a time. Even advanced philosophers have to proceed that way.

Woman: But I've known people who can only talk about one thing at a time. They're not very good conversationalists. A good conversation can jump around. *We're* jumping around today.

Director: That's because we're *comfortable* jumping around. And sometimes a jump shakes loose a bad idea.

Woman: Why are we comfortable?

Director: Because we haven't spoken of much to make us uncomfortable.

Woman: Don't you want to make me uncomfortable to see where I need work?

Director: Discomfort is adjacent to comfort many times. So when we land on the comfortable, we'll know what's next door—and make a mental note to return to it one day.

Woman: The contrast helps show things for what they are.

Director: Yes. Philosophers deal in contrast. But people often believe the contrasting thing is wrong.

WRONG

Woman: Wait, are you saying people sometimes believe comfort is wrong?

Director: Certain people do. They sometimes take pride in their discomfort. It takes an effort to be uncomfortable and carry on. Surely there's a reward for this endurance. That's how they think.

Woman: Is there a reward? Because if not, I think it's tragic.

Director: Well, learning how to endure can be good. The question is— endure *what*?

Woman: There has to be a reason to endure. What's a good reason to endure?

Director: To overcome wrong.

Woman: I agree. But some wrong is never-ending, you know. You can endure for a while, but when you get the sense that nothing will change—you have to separate yourself from the wrong.

Director: This is true. How you think we know when enough is enough?

Woman: Something inside tells us it's time to go. I don't know what that something is. It's just a feeling you get, and when you couple it with a long history of endurance, you know.

Director: Sometimes leaving is for the best not only for you. The one in the wrong is often shocked when we leave. Sometimes this causes them to reflect. And sometimes this reflection urges them to change.

Woman: And sometimes they change. That's a lot of *sometimes*.

Director: Yes, people don't change very often. To be more clear—people seldom change.

Woman: Very few change. Yes. But what if they don't need to change? What if right from birth they're on the right track?

Director: They are very lucky. This happens now and then. They never seem to be in the wrong. Sure, occasionally they are—they're human, of course. But in the main they're used to being in the right.

Woman: And they're very comfortable with that.

Director: No, not always. It can be uncomfortable to be in the right when you're surrounded by those in the wrong.

Woman: But that's why people like this stick together. They surround themselves with people in the right.

Director: True, they certainly try to do this with all their might. Do you know people like this?

Woman: I do—and they're insufferable!

Director: Why?

Woman: Because as you suggested, it's inhuman to always be in the right— or even to come close!

Director: You prefer those who are in the wrong?

Woman: I think we need to get clear on what is right and what is wrong. Right is correct, proper—priggish. Wrong is... human!

Director: Okay. I think I know what you're getting at. But I don't like to say wrong is right, if you know what I mean. I prefer the human way of right.

Woman: Rightness with a soft edge?

Director: Pliable rightness.

Woman: Well, *pliable* makes rightness sound weak. Maybe flexible?

Director: Flexible, sure. Able to adapt.

Woman: Tolerant?

Director: That's an interesting question. Should right tolerate wrong? I want to say no. But maybe right tolerates forgivable failings.

Woman: What's an example of a forgivable failing?

Director: Something where no one gets hurt. And I don't want to talk about butterfly effects and that sort of thing. I'm talking about something where we can see someone getting hurt.

Woman: If no gets hurt by the wrong, let it slide?

Director: I'm not so sure I want to take the credit for that advice.

ADVICE

Woman: Would you rather say you should cut people a little slack?

Director: That does sound better, and I think it's good to give some slack. Life is hard enough as it is without having to be perfect all the time.

Woman: That's what good conductors do. They don't aim for perfection. They give the orchestra a little room to breathe.

Director: Room to breathe sounds nice. That's the advice I'd give. Allow some room to breathe. We all have to breathe, after all.

Woman: What's *breath* to a philosopher?

Director: Thought. Thinking is mental breathing, you know.

Woman: Too bad more people don't have mental do not resuscitate orders! You don't waste time trying to resuscitate the mentally dead, do you?

Director: If it's clear they've stopped all thought, I have nothing to do with them. But if they are trying, no matter how bad they are, I would try as well.

Woman: But what does it mean for you to try? Do you invest much time?

Director: These things don't always take a lot of time. A choice word spoken here and there can work wonders—or at least it can encourage further thought.

Woman: But thought towards what end?

Director: Self-sustaining life. And when you achieve self-sustaining life, you arrive at a degree of mental and spiritual comfort you've never known before.

Woman: Then I must not yet be self-sustaining. But I thought you said you were still a work in progress.

Director: You can't work unless you're alive. And you can take comfort in the work, even if it's uncomfortable.

Woman: Comfort in the uncomfortable? How does that work? Or is this just some paradox I have to accept?

Director: The work might be uncomfortable, but you know it's for your own good. So you take comfort in that knowledge even though another part of you is in discomfort.

Woman: Ah, parts. But how do you *know* it's for your own good? Shouldn't we say you trust or believe?

Director: You have a point. But when you trust, you base it on past experience which is a guide. You consider it very likely your effort will pay off.

Woman: Making you even more comfortable?

Director: If that's what you want, sure.

Woman: What else could we want?

Director: Knowledge, understanding. Things like that.

Woman: But aren't those things comforting to have?

Director: They can be. But they can also lead to increased desire to have more. So you prepare yourself for more work, more discomfort.

Woman: But you can choose when you work, right?

Director: Sometimes the work chooses us. Knowledge can be very demanding, jealous of our time. Understanding is often worse.

Woman: I think I know what you mean about understanding. It gnaws at you until you give in and think it through. So what do you advise? Give in at once?

Director: You need to find time alone where you can really think. If you try to think in crowded mental space you'll only confuse things and make it worse.

Woman: But what do I do if I'm in the middle of a very demanding time at work? I have no time to myself, barely to even sleep.

Director: This is where you have to endure in discomfort until you can find the time.

Woman: Endurance, yes. But won't I seem distracted?

Director: You probably will. And it will probably affect your job. Best to find the time as quickly as you can. Take a sick day or two. Do what you must. It's a matter of priority.

Woman: Mental health versus work. You're saying I should choose mental health.

Director: Doesn't that seem like good advice?

Woman: It seems like the only advice there can be. No one would come out and say choose work over your mental health.

Director: Yes, but it often goes unsaid.

UNSAID

Woman: Lots goes unsaid in this world. Why do you think that is?

Director: Because it's not easy to say you want to have your cake and eat it, too. That's one reason, I think. Another reason is that certain things are ugly when spoken aloud. We tend to keep the ugly in the dark.

Woman: I know you're not talking about this, but it reminds me of how we treat ugly people. I can't imagine how horrible it is to be ugly. Think of when we were kids. What torments the ugly endured.

Director: I take it you're not speaking of ugly in soul. You mean beauty of appearance. Looks.

Woman: Yes. You know how shallow people are. They're sweet to the good looking and don't give the ugly the time of day.

Director: Imagine what you could learn about how the world works if you were ugly.

Woman: It would be the inverse of what the beautiful learn. And yet for all this learning precious little is said.

Director: I know what you mean. But, then again, there's nothing we talk about more. How many plots revolve around the dynamic of ugly versus beautiful. In fact, I've seen so many I sometimes get confused.

Woman: What are you talking about?

Director: Some people think eagles are beautiful, birds of prey. Others think bunny rabbits are beautiful, eagles' prey.

Woman: They're both beautiful in their own way. But let's talk about humans. I'm attracted to the quirky in looks. Forget about *classical* beauty. Who needs that? It's boring. What about you?

Director: I, too, appreciate quirks in looks. But the reason I do is that the heart-mind-soul collective animates the looks.

Woman: The heart-mind-soul collective. That's funny. That's a term for our humanity.

Director: Yes. Take a classical beauty, throw in some quirky humanity, and I think it's hard to beat. And I'll make a prediction. Such a person would not be perceived as classically beautiful.

Woman: Because of the way they act?

Director: Yes.

Woman: I don't know, Director. Looks are hard to play down. Classical beauty is classical beauty.

Director: Maybe in photography or painted portraits. But put the person in play, and I think they'll scare some admirers off.

Woman: I don't think you're shallow enough to understand that you're wrong.

Director: I don't think you're experienced enough to know that I'm right.

Woman: Ha! That may be. We'll have to put it to the test. Do you know anyone with classical beauty who has serious quirks?

Director: I once knew someone, yes.

Woman: What happened to him?

Director: He was torn to pieces by a mob in Egypt.

Woman: I'm sorry. I had no idea. People are so awful.

Director: I think it was hard on him because his physical beauty set high expectations among certain others. But then when he opened his mouth to speak—trouble.

Woman: He didn't buy into his beauty.

Director: You put that exactly right. Was that a flaw?

Woman: I'm someone who thinks flaws make beauty more precious. So he wouldn't leave the unsayable unsaid?

Director: Nope. He said it all. It cost him his life. He wasn't overly prudent, we might say.

Woman: Why are people so afraid of death?

Director: It's the great unknown. People are afraid of what they don't know.

Woman: Aren't you?

Director: I try to know what I don't. There's an old saying that philosophy means learning how to die.

Woman: Have you learned? I know I haven't. I want a good death. But if it comes on me in a bad way, I'm not sure I'd do so well. I want death on my terms.

SUICIDE

Director: Suicide is death on your terms. Is that what you mean?

Woman: I.... No, that's not what I mean. I mean I want to be prepared. How does philosophy prepare you?

Director: I'm not sure it does.

Woman: But you just said!

Director: It's an old saying. Sayings aren't always true. I try to learn how to die, but how would I know if I know how? There's only one test. And maybe it's not such a big deal. Maybe we all fumble our way into death.

Woman: What about Socrates? He knew how to die.

Director: Did he? I don't know. Plato could have been a pretty big liar. Maybe he portrayed Socrates as more sure of himself than he was. Plato wasn't even there when he died. Have you ever seen someone die?

Woman: Animals, yes. A human? No. Have you?

Director: I've seen both. They're very much the same, at the actual moment.

Woman: Animals don't commit suicide.

Director: That's one of the clear ways in which we differ. Why do you think that is?

Woman: Well, why do people commit suicide? Often it's because they feel that life has no meaning. Animals must have a sense of meaning.

Director: That or meaning means nothing to them. They just are.

Woman: I wish I could just be. Have you ever wanted to kill yourself?

Director: I suppose if I really wanted to I would have. But if you're asking if I ever fell on black days—yes, of course.

Woman: What did you do to get out?

Director: I'm not sure. I either waited for the sun to rise; or I kept on moving forward if only in a crawl. Maybe I was crawling toward the dawn.

Woman: Crawling toward the dawn. It sounds like the name of a book or a song. Which would you rather it be?

Director: I have a question before I answer. What usually happens? Do writers get inspired to write by a song; or do composers get inspired to compose by a book?

Woman: I think it happens often both ways.

Director: Then it doesn't matter if my catchy phrase is used one way or another.

Woman: When the dawn came, all was well?

Director: That's what the metaphor says.

Woman: But what do you say?

Director: Do you know how desperate you have to be for the sun, to crawl toward the east in hopes this will bring light even if only milliseconds sooner? Can you imagine?

Woman: I don't have to imagine. I've been there. But why exhaust yourself in crawling? Why not grow patient and wait in one spot?

Director: Is that what you do?

Woman: It is. I meditate.

Director: I've tried that. It doesn't work for me. When things aren't so bad I run to the east. Running sometimes lifts my spirits.

Woman: Why do your spirits grow black?

Director: I really don't know.

Woman: Have you tried going to a therapist?

Director: I have. But she needed therapy more than I.

Woman: Yes, but that doesn't mean she can't help. I've been to therapy. I still go now and then.

Director: Does it help ?

Woman: I don't know. So why do I go? Maybe it's my form of doing the crawl.

DAYLIGHT

Director: But do you know what's funny? When I make it to daylight, sometime in the afternoon I long for the night.

Woman: I love the night. I always have. I also love the rain. It's a sort of daytime night. What do you think that says about me?

Director: You have less need for daylight than many.

Woman: Less need than you?

Director: I can manage on very little light. But I enjoy many things in the light.

Woman: What kind of things?

Director: I love to hike. What do you love to do in the light?

Woman: I love to hike on rainy days. What else do you love to do in the light?

Director: I love to have stirring conversations.

Woman: I love to have stirring conversations when sheltered from the rain. Why do you love conversations in the daylight?

Director: Daylight encourages truthfulness.

Woman: Oh, that's not true. My cloudy rainy days support plenty of truth. But let me tell you a secret, one I've never told anyone else.

Director: Are you sure you want to?

Woman: Don't be silly. I started liking the rain as a kid—because all the other kids couldn't come out and play. What do you think of that?

Director: You wanted to be alone?

Woman: Yes, and when it's sunny and nice everyone comes around to play. But when it rains, they stay in—in their own homes, away from me.

Director: You were an only child.

Woman: Were? Am. But it's your turn. You said you long for the night. Why?

Director: The day is done; people retire to their homes; I go to mine and enjoy my solitude.

Woman: There's something about it when you say it, something... final. What do you do in your solitude?

Director: I read; sometimes I write; sometimes I just think.

Woman: And sometimes you watch tv! I know you.

Director: True, I enjoy a good show.

Woman: Don't you ever get lonely?

Director: Yes, I do.

Woman: I do, too. Why don't you do something about it?

Director: What's to be done?

Woman: Not you're the fatalist. How about finding a wife? That would keep you in company.

Director: I don't want to be in company. Most of the time I enjoy my solitude just fine. Is it fair to someone to say, 'Hey, be with me now and then, when I'm feeling lonely'?

Woman: No, you have a point. That's not fair. So you really think you'll be a bachelor the rest of your life?

Director: I'm open to being wrong—but yes. How about you?

Woman: I'm going to be an old maid. I can just never find anyone I like.

Director: Do you encounter these *anyones* in broad daylight or in the rain?

Woman: Does it matter?

Director: I'm just saying that you need to have a good look before you decide.

Woman: And what should I look for? What's the most important thing in a relationship? Being comfortable with one another? Is that it?

Director: Maybe. Some people look for growth. But growth isn't always pleasant. Growth can hurt. How about something like that?

Woman: No thanks. I'll find ways to grow on my own.

PAIN

Director: Growth will still involve pain.

Woman: Better to suffer on my own. Isn't that how you think?

Director: It is. I try hardest when I'm alone.

Woman: You try to grow out of your pain. Or should I say you try to grow *from* your pain? Maybe you don't want to get rid of the pain. Maybe you'd miss your pain. Have you always had pain?

Director: Have you? Pain is a background thing. We don't let it get right up front. Not letting it do that is how we grow. We develop muscles to push the pain back.

Woman: I'm not as strong as I'd like. My pain often pushes its way right up. What can I do?

Director: Take a step back, so the pain is forced to step back, too. Then quickly take several steps forward. The pain might catch back up, but you've bought yourself some time.

Woman: Is this what it comes to in life? Buying ourselves a little time? I suppose it's better than having no time away from pain. But it just seems so sad.

Director: Buying time is victory. Time is the only currency in life. We must take as much of it as we can. It's not sad. It's what we do.

Woman: It still seems sad. Are we really thieves of time? Do we steal time however we can?

Director: Pain is the thief—or robber, I should say. It threatens and uses force when it will.

Woman: We should focus on getting rid of the pain. Or are you going to tell me *no pain, no gain?*

Director: There's truth to that saying. And the gain when it comes to the spirit is growth.

Woman: What does it mean to grow in spirit?

Director: To increase in knowledge and understanding.

Woman: My father told me to know few things but to know them very well. I'm not sure if that applies to understanding, but I'm inclined to say yes.

Director: I agree with your father. Growth takes a very long time. It's true there can be bursts, but slow growth is the rule. In that slow growth there's no time to know a great many things. Your father was wise. We know what we can. In the end it is isn't that much.

Woman: Great, all this pain with little to show.

Director: But show whom? You will know you've grown. And you know many, most perhaps, don't grow at all.

Woman: So you want me to compare myself to them? That's my victory? I've grown more than the slugs?

Director: The victory is that you'll enjoy being you—despite any pain. Pain really should be a background thing. Don't let it disturb your pleasure. In fact, by way of high relief, let it enhance your pleasure.

Woman: Can you imagine a life with no pain?

Director: Sure, it's the life of the slugs. No growth.

Woman: What's so good about growth?

Director: It can give meaning. It satisfies. Or don't you agree?

Woman: I suppose I have to agree—or what am I? Pain in life is a fact. There's no getting around it. But I'm not prepared for more pain here today.

Director: Our friends are in good hands. Their surgeries were necessary. All we can do now is hope for the best.

Woman: I don't want to grow at the cost of my friend's life. I'd rather be a slug when it comes to this.

Director: Your friend wouldn't want you to grow?

Woman: I'm just saying I don't want her to die. There are plenty of other opportunities for pain in life.

Director: That there are. So we're in luck.

Woman: Do you think those without much pain are unlucky?

Director: Lucky in one sense, unlucky in another. They have no opportunity.

Woman: That's the promise of this country—opportunity. And it keeps the promise.

COMFORTING

Director: How do we know the idea of growth isn't just a comforting thought?

Woman: It's like you said. We gain in knowledge and understanding. Those are very real things.

Director: How do we know knowledge and understanding aren't just ways of comforting ourselves?

Woman: If they are, they're good ways. But I don't think they are. People comfort themselves in other ways. Usually by refusing to think.

Director: That's a mistake. When prompted to think, we should think. If we don't...

Woman: ...things begin to fester. We need to let that sunlight in.

Director: Is festering comfortable? I don't think I could get comfortable in fester.

Woman: You'd be surprised what some people get comfortable in. Pigs are very comfortable in their sties. But humans aren't pigs. They don't belong in a sty.

Director: Why do humans go where they don't belong? Or another way of asking—where do humans belong? In the light.

Woman: Well, you know I love rain. Am I not going where I belong?

Director: What does it mean to say, 'You belong here'?

Woman: It means you think you know better than them.

Director: Do we know better? Isn't it up to each of us to judge?

Woman: So, what? Human beings only belong where they think they belong? Anything goes?

Director: Would you rather live in a world where you're told where you belong?

Woman: I live in that world now. My family tries to tell me where I belong. My bosses at work try to tell me where I belong. Even my friends try to tell me where I belong.

Director: Are you where you belong?

Woman: I love what I do. And because it's prestigious, most people leave me alone.

Director: Ah, prestige. Prestige means you're where most people think you should be.

Woman: The second chair doesn't always agree. But I would say it's a little different. Prestige is when you're where most people think they might like to be. Prestige is when you're somewhere they think must be good.

Director: You command respect because of this?

Woman: Yes.

Director: Do you like to command respect?

Woman: I like respect, but I don't like to command it. I don't like to command.

Director: Shouldn't leaders be comfortable in command? You're a leader in your role.

Woman: You can lead without giving commands. You can express your desire and then explain. That goes over better than command.

Director: If you're talking to people who are willing to listen, sure. Does everyone at work listen?

Woman: More or less? Yes. I guess I have a lucky job.

Director: I guess you do. My team doesn't always listen. And so I have to command.

Woman: Do you hate commanding?

Director: No, I don't mind. I give people a chance to listen. If they don't, it's no trouble to command.

Woman: It's trouble for me. I'm very uncomfortable giving commands.

Director: 'Play it this way; don't play it like that'?

Woman: Things like that, yes. But I'll tell you the truth. I rely on the conductor to help.

Director: Ah, external forces. That always comes at a cost. What's the price you pay?

Woman: The ones who don't agree with me think I'm weak.

Director: Are you weak?

Woman: In these things I am.

Director: So why not grow into command? Drop reliance on the conductor to help.

Woman: I worry they'll hate me if I command.

HATE

Director: I would think they'd hate you more if you rely on the conductor to help.

Woman: Why?

Director: Because it shows you're weak. And maybe I was wrong. Maybe it's not hate. Maybe they despise you for not dealing with things yourself.

Woman: You might be right. But what a choice! Be hated or despised. Hate seems more honest, no?

Director: I would rather be hated than despised. I don't like to be an object of contempt. But there are tactical considerations here.

Woman: Like what will keep me my job?

Director: Sure. Or what will most effectively crush the resistance you face. The conductor might do it best.

Woman: And then they'll hate the conductor and despise me. But I'm making things sound so bad! They're really not that bad. I work with wonderful people.

Director: Even wonderful people can live comfortably in their own sties. But tell me something. Are wonderful people uncomfortable with themselves?

Woman: That's a good question. I think the answer is no. Or, then again, maybe they can be.

Director: How?

Woman: They're wonderful to others because they're covering up their discomfort.

Director: Does it work? Does it make them feel good?

Woman: Cover-ups never work. In fact, I think they make things worse.

Director: Do you cover up?

Woman: I do.

Director: Why? And what can you do?

Woman: Why? I don't know. What can I do? I can be more honest. And, as a result, maybe be more hated.

Director: Is being hated such a terrible thing? Everyone seems to think it's the worst thing on Earth. What happens when you're hated?

Woman: People make things difficult for you.

Director: Is difficulty the worst thing on Earth?

Woman: Life is difficult enough, don't you think?

Director: Life can be difficult, yes. But if you can be comfortable with yourself....

Woman: While you're hated? How can that be?

Director: Like you said, you're more honest. Honesty should be a comfortable thing. Yes?

Woman: True. But no one can be wholly honest, no one who isn't a fool.

Director: Be more honest, yes. I bet you'll feel better about yourself.

Woman: And those whose feelings I hurt? Because, you know, I will hurt people's feelings if I say what I really think.

Director: Pick and choose whom to hurt. Experiment a bit. See what you can learn.

Woman: Experiment? Experiment on living souls?

Director: I was thinking you'd experiment on yourself. That's what we're concerned with here. If people can't handle a little honesty, what can we say?

Woman: A little honesty, yes. I'll start out small. Then I can learn. Then I can grow. No one hates anyone over a little honesty, right?

Director: Of course they do. They might even hate you more. If you are completely honest, they might come to fear you more than hate.

Woman: I don't want to be feared!

Director: Why not? Is being feared so bad? If fear can override hate, I would say it's a good thing. The hateful are more inclined to attack, to make things difficult for you.

Woman: You're saying halfway measures are no good.

Director: They are no good. Maybe good for learning a lesson. But no, no good.

Woman: If only people knew what goes on behind the scenes in an orchestra....

Director: They might not be so surprised. They have their own backstage, too.

BACKSTAGE

Woman: You never know what's in the backstage of a life.

Director: You might not know what, but you might see that something is wrong.

Woman: Because they're uncomfortable with themselves?

Director: Well, that raises an interesting question. Can you appear comfortable while having much backstage nonsense going on?

Woman: I think you can. People can be good actors. I know I am. Are you?

Director: I don't think I am. I don't want the backstage problems to establish themselves while I'm busy acting away. I leave the stage, no matter the performance, and deal with them the best I can. And if that means I'm off stage for a good long while, so be it.

Woman: But what does that mean? How can you just go off stage? The stage is where we live. Have you heard all the world's a stage?

Director: Then backstage is a stage, too.

Woman: I never thought of that. You're right. But I'm a little uncomfortable with all of this.

Director: Why? What's wrong?

Woman: All the world's a stage means someone is watching what we do—even when we're alone. So who does the watching then? God?

Director: Maybe all it means is that what we do when we're alone can been seen by those with eyes to see.

Woman: That sounds creepy. You'd better say more.

Director: It just means, for instance, if you love to read when you're alone, I might be able to see that in you. What we do when we're alone shapes our character. And character is there for all to see.

Woman: Well, that's not creepy at all. It's true. I like people who love to read.

Director: Does it matter what they read?

Woman: Not really. Reading as reading is good, if you ask me.

Director: What is it about reading? I like to read philosophy, but I also like to read detective stories. What does that say about me?

Woman: Don't ask two questions at once. That's probably a bad habit you learned from all those philosophy books. What is it about reading? You have to make an effort to understand.

Director: But what if the author has played to the crowd and made it so there's nothing new to understand? Good guys are good; bad guys are bad.

Woman: Sure, I know what you mean. That's why there have to be literary breakthroughs every now and again. Breakthrough books take work to understand.

Director: And then a generation of literary followers sprouts right up.

Woman: A new genre is born.

Director: It doesn't happen very often.

Woman: Would you consider philosophy a genre?

Director: Yes, there are those who simply follow suit; no, that's not the kind of philosophy I read.

Woman: Let me guess. You read the masters. But how do you know they're really masters? How do you know they didn't play to the crowd.

Director: It's hard to say. There's something about them that makes this clear. Usually it's something that's not.

Woman: Something that's *not*? It's hard to prove a negative.

Director: Very hard. That's why most people aren't very good judges of what philosophy isn't.

Woman: So if you rule out everything else, philosophy is what's left?

Director: I think that's fair to say. And then you put it to the test.

Woman: How?

Director: You ask questions of the book and listen closely for the answer.

Woman: What kind of questions?

Director: Questions about the backstage of the author's life.

BIOGRAPHY

Woman: You hunt for biography?

Director: Biography informs what philosophers say. But philosophers jealously guard information about their backstage.

Woman: Most people do. We share it with friends.

Director: Yes, and that's why there are philosophical circles. Friends of the circle share.

Woman: Personal life should be personal life—for everyone. Everything is fair game for everyone only if you become... famous. Then everyone thinks they have a right to know.

Director: First chair violinists at a symphony like ours aren't famous?

Woman: I admit I have a fair amount of fame in music circles.

Director: I wouldn't know. Are you comfortable with your fame?

Woman: I smile a lot. I help raise a lot of money. I teach kids how to play from time to time. Do I like the expectations on me? No. Could I do without the fame? Yes. I just love to play.

Director: Did you always love to play?

Woman: From the time I was a very little girl. The violin just always made sense to me somehow. Did you always love philosophy?

Director: I think I did.

Woman: What do you mean? You *think*?

Director: I didn't know what philosophy was until I was older. When I learned what it was, I realized—that's what I am, a philosopher. Though I sometimes have my doubts.

Woman: What doubts? You're the most philosophical person I've ever met.

Director: I doubt whether I'm philosopher enough, whether I'm too much of a coward to see philosophy through.

Woman: It can be scary to learn and grow.

Director: At times it can be very scary, yes. But it can also be difficult when you have to stand up to someone and say, 'No, that's not true.' Depending on the circumstances, that can land you in a lot of trouble. I admit I sometimes shy away from trouble.

Woman: Who doesn't! I could have trouble every day if I wanted it. I don't. Does that make me a coward? Maybe. But then all but the insane are cowards. Don't be too hard on yourself.

Director: Well, that sounds like good advice. But don't you be too hard on yourself either, with all the smiling that you do.

Woman: How is that being hard? If anything it's a coward's smile.

Director: You're hard on yourself in that you want to be well loved.

Woman: No, that's not really it. I smile because I'm afraid of what people will think if they know who I really am.

Director: Who you really are is someone who smiles a lot.

Woman: That's a bucket of cold water on the head. You don't think there's more to me than that?

Director: Of course I do. But as far as others know, that's who you are— the smiling first chair. But let me guess something. You don't smile when you play.

Woman: How did you know? I've never, from the time I was very young, smiled while playing. Why do you think that is?

Director: Because when you play you're in touch with yourself, and that is your sacred oasis.

Woman: Oasis, yes. But sacred? I'll have to think about that. I want to agree but something about it doesn't sit well.

Director: Sacred just means worthy of veneration. To venerate means to show great respect. Do you have a problem with self-respect?

Woman: I... might. Can you say more?

Director: Fools can have self-respect. Maybe your problem lies along these lines.

Woman: Yes, I've noticed that sometimes the biggest idiot has the most respect for himself. It's comical.

Director: Are you afraid you'll be a comical idiot if you have a great deal of self-respect?

Woman: Maybe I am.

FLOW

Director: I go back and forth. Sometimes I venerate myself and I soon feel like a fool. Other times I don't pay myself any attention at all and seem to get along just fine.

Woman: When are the times you don't pay any attention? What are you doing?

Director: Some people call it flow. I'm flowing. When I flow I don't worry about self-respect.

Woman: That makes sense! When you flow you don't have time for anything else. So how do we flow?

Director: Do you ski?

Woman: Not often, but yes.

Director: Imagine you had no lift to take you to the top of the mountain. You have to climb up on your own. That would take some work, no? That's what it's like with flow. You do a great deal of work, then you have a short run.

Woman: Some people make it sound like they flow all the time.

Director: It isn't that way with me. I doubt it's that way with them.

Woman: Do you think they're acting?

Director: I do. And they may even have themselves fooled.

Woman: Why pretend to flow? People respect hard work and admire occasional flow.

Director: These people are probably flow coaches, flow consultants, what have you. They have an interest in knowing flow. And how can you know if you don't flow?

Woman: You're probably right. But if they're not flowing, if they're pretending—doesn't the question of self-respect arise?

Director: They pretend they have self-respect. Once you start pretending, the limits are few.

Woman: I believe it. Does philosophy flow?

Director: When it's in the right conversation, it does.

Woman: You seem to be flowing here with me.

Director: And you seem to be flowing with me. But, you know, I've had a hundred bad conversations, conversations that were uphill work, before I got to this one.

Woman: I've had more like a thousand.

Director: Even so, it all seems worth it—doesn't it?

Woman: I'm enjoying our conversation. But I have to be honest with you. A thousand bad conversations is much to ask. What happens when our friends are better and we go home. Another thousand for me?

Director: Maybe.

Woman: An honest answer. I can't bear the thought of all that uphill work. I think I'll just remain silent. After all, I didn't do much work before today and here I am flowing with you.

Director: Silence can be a kind of work. Do you find it easy to remain silent?

Woman: I don't. I often want to scream.

Director: Maybe silence is your work. I don't know. I know it's not mine, though I do know how to be silent at times.

Woman: Why do you think you're one way and I'm another?

Director: Who can say? But the silent can be strong—a rock washed over by waves of speech. That's resistance.

Woman: But who wants to be a rock? It makes me think of rocks in the head.

Director: Well, yes. There isn't much thought in being a rock.

Woman: And that's why you speak in your struggle uphill. You think and then you feel compelled to say.

Director: Not always. But for the most part? Yes, I think then I want to speak. I want to communicate my thoughts. That takes some tact, as you might guess. But out it comes.

Woman: I think you're healthier for it. Keeping bottled up is no good.

Director: Do you ever communicate your thoughts?

Woman: I journal. It keeps me sane.

YOURSELF 2

Director: Would you ever publish your journals? I think there would be an audience for that.

Woman: Why would I want to do that? My most private thoughts? Shared with the world? No thanks.

Director: You'll remain the rock until the end. Or, we could see the rock bloom into a flower.

Woman: Thinking I'd publish someday would inhibit my thoughts. A journal is no good unless you can be free.

Director: Publish after you're dead. Name a literary executor in your will.

Woman: But why would I do it? It does nothing for me after I'm dead.

Director: But it might do something for someone else—someone like you. Don't you think it would be worth it if just one person read what you wrote and took courage from it?

Woman: If I inspired someone? Well, you have a point. But right now I'm writing for no one but me.

Director: This person will be like you. So keep writing for yourself.

Woman: But isn't the first rule of writing to know your audience?

Director: You can discover who you are as you write.

Woman: You know, I flow when I write. I'm not paying attention to who I am.

Director: What do you write?

Woman: Observations on others. Who they are; what they do; what they like. Can you see what a disaster publishing that would be?

Director: I can see it might cause an explosion. Do you like explosions?

Woman: I like fireworks.

Director: This will certainly cause some. Do you believe in an afterlife?

Woman: I don't. But that doesn't mean there isn't one.

Director: Well, you would have a front row seat for the show.

Woman: You know, as I lay dying that might comfort me. But wouldn't it show my life to have been a lie?

Director: The sphinx doesn't speak. Does that make it a liar?

Woman: No, it makes it a sphinx. You'd have me turn from a rock into a sphinx.

Director: You might be more satisfied with yourself this way. And others might sense a sort of power in you. Wouldn't you like to seem powerful?

Woman: This would give me a sense of power. I'd like that. The power to say whatever I want about the many fools and worse in the world.

Director: In another age we'd say you'd have sand.

Woman: Stubbornness? No, purpose. My purpose is to say it like it is. I can live with that. It's good to have a purpose. I don't have a real purpose now. Sure, my career. But I've never thought of that as my purpose in life. Playing is what I love.

Director: But what we love can give us purpose—purpose to do what we love.

Woman: I want to be on a mission.

Director: Why?

Woman: What do you mean, 'Why?' I want to be dedicated to the cause of truth.

Director: Do you think we all need a cause?

Woman: No, most people just live. Only a few live for a cause outside themselves.

Director: I'm not sure about this cause business. Causes can blind us in important ways.

Woman: Maybe we need to be blind in an important way.

Director: Can you say more?

Woman: Blindness to ourselves. You've hinted at this. Maybe it's necessary to live life the way we should. We put ourselves in our blind spot—and we all have a blind spot—and we flow when we can. I'll flow when I write. And when I observe others, I'll be more patient because I know when I get home I'll flow once again.

Director: That sounds like a good plan. But there's one thing. You'll have more to write about if you break your silence and speak. As you interact you'll see more things.

Woman: Not necessarily. Don't you know? The fly on the wall sees it all.

SEEING

Director: But you're not a fly. You're first chair violin in a world renowned orchestra.

Woman: What more do you think I'll see if I speak?

Director: Silence from someone like you can intimidate others. If you speak a little you might allow them to open up.

Woman: But I don't need them to open up. I already know what's inside.

Director: How do you know?

Woman: I see how they interact with others. I see how they interact with me. I can guess what's inside.

Director: So when you write in your journal you say, 'I guess so-and-so is like this'? Wouldn't it be better to be able to say, 'So-and-so is like this—and here's why'?

Woman: Do you think knowing is always better than guessing?

Director: I don't. There are some things we don't need to know. But if you're writing about people I think you should know.

Woman: Okay. I'll try and open them up a little bit more. But I'm going to dip my toe in the water first before I go all the way in—*if* I go all the way in.

Director: A toe in the water might be all you need to see some for what they are. But for others you may have to go all the way in.

Woman: Tell me something. Are we having an all-the-way-in conversation now? I think I have a pretty good idea of who you are. Do you have a pretty good idea of who I am?

Director: I think I do. I think I can see much of who you are.

Woman: Yes, but only *much*? Don't you want to see all?

Director: I'm not sure I can. I'd have to walk a mile in your shoes. Do you know what I mean?

Woman: Of course I know what you mean. And I'm not sure I could walk a mile in your shoes. Philosophy isn't my thing. Yes, I can have a conversation like this with you; no, I can't initiate one with others.

Director: You just have to try. You might be surprised how quickly you can learn.

Woman: Maybe. But the problem is I don't *want* to walk a mile in most people's shoes. The thought of it disgusts me, if I'm honest with you. And I bet you agree.

Director: I don't want to know everyone. True. There's only so much time and energy in life.

Woman: And that's the thing.

Director: But being silent takes its toll, doesn't it? Doesn't being silent exhaust you some of the time?

Woman: Much of the time.

Director: Speaking a little can give you a lift.

Woman: Yes, but speaking what? Nonsense like most other people speak?

Director: Do they know it's nonsense?

Woman: I think most of them must. I think they speak it because they have to have something to say. Not I.

Director: You're too proud to speak nonsense.

Woman: Is there something wrong with that?

Director: If it wears you out, maybe. Maybe you should try a little nonsense and see how it goes.

Woman: But that would be so out of character that everyone would look to see what's wrong.

Director: And what's wrong?

Woman: Nothing. But they will talk.

Director: Let them talk. A rock can take a little talk. A rock with a flower growing from one of the cracks can—

Woman: But that's the thing! They'll think I cracked.

Director: Sometimes it's good to let them think you're a little nuts.

CRAZY

Woman: Do people think you're a little nuts?

Director: Oh yes, definitely.

Woman: Why? Because you're a philosopher?

Director: People read about philosophy and think it's fine, innocent, harmless. But if they ever meet a philosopher....

Woman: What do you mean?

Director: It takes imagination and insight to see philosophy for what it was in ages gone by. We think of gentle Socrates more often than not. But we forget there was a reason he was put to death.

Woman: What was the reason?

Director: He talked too much from inside.

Woman: He would have been better off as a rock.

Director: Maybe he just couldn't stay silent. Ancient Athens was a crazy place. Keeping silent may have amounted to consent, approval of all he saw.

Woman: Do you think I approve of all I see?

Director: No, I'm sure you don't. But don't let your disapproval drive you nuts.

Woman: How would it do that?

Director: It might back you into a corner. Philosophers stay out of the corners. This drives some people mad.

Woman: Maybe they killed Socrates because he wouldn't let them corner him.

Director: That might be.

Woman: Do philosophers secretly want to be killed?

Director: In my opinion Socrates did. I don't know about the others.

Woman: How can I become a philosopher?

Director: Ask that question in earnest and learn as you go.

Woman: There's no formula to follow? No path to trod?

Director: Nope. You have to do it all on your own.

Woman: That sounds very hard.

Director: Life can be very hard no matter what you are. Given that, I choose the difficulty of philosophy.

Woman: What's the purpose of philosophy?

Director: What's the cause? That's something you have to come up with on your own.

Woman: So you admit there's a cause.

Director: I believe some philosophers see philosophy as a cause. Do I? Sometimes.

Woman: But a cause isn't a cause if it's only *sometimes*.

Director: Maybe it's not a very good cause.

Woman: How can you say that? If something is your cause, you...

Director: ...venerate it? At times I do. At times I think I'm nuts.

Woman: Sometimes when I'm silent too long I start to think I'm crazy. And I'm not talking about being a mute. I talk about what we need to do when I'm at work. I talk to the violinists. I talk to the conductor. I talk to donors. But I don't really talk. I'm not talking, if you know what I mean.

Director: Philosophers know how to keep silent in an ocean of speech. So yes, I know what you mean. You want your words to come from the heart. You want them to count. I think I understand.

Woman: You do understand. The only real words I'll speak will be in my journal.

Director: But dipping your toe means you speak a little from the heart.

Woman: Yes, but if I do—I'm afraid they'll think I'm nuts.

SANITY

Director: What does it mean to be nuts?

Woman: Not to think like everyone thinks.

Director: Does everyone really think the same way?

Woman: The majority do, sure.

Director: Then the minority might not think you're nuts.

Woman: But what if I'm unique? Everyone will think I'm nuts.

Director: Maybe it's as simple as that. If you want to be unique, you risk your sanity.

Woman: How does that work?

Director: You can be sane and unique at once. But the problem is others might think you're insane—and you might come to think that way, too.

Woman: You have to be a rock. But if everyone thinks you're insane, aren't you insane?

Director: What is sanity?

Woman: Thinking like everyone else.

Director: So every genius discoverer was insane?

Woman: I want to say yes. But let's be clear. We're not talking about clinical madness—hallucinations and the like.

Director: No, that's just being sick, not being nuts. For sickness there can be a cure, if you're lucky. But for real insanity? The only way out is through.

Woman: And that's exactly what terrifies me. But through to what?

Director: Mental health. You can be crazy and healthy, too.

Woman: Yes, but you don't really mean *crazy*. You mean 'crazy'. Right?

Director: Well, if crazy is not thinking like everyone else, no—crazy is crazy. It's crazy not to think like everyone else. No doubt about it.

Woman: Then I am crazy. You are crazy. All the philosophers there ever were were crazy.

Director: But do you know how they regain their sanity?

Woman: Tell me.

Director: They make others think like them.

Woman: That's the through.

Director: That's the through. Getting others to see your truth is very hard.

Woman: Philosophical circles.

Director: What do you mean?

Woman: Within your circle where people think like you, you're sane. Outside the circle you're still nuts. That's why circles form.

Director: Yes, you have a point.

Woman: We help each other. Maybe there are people I can help, who can help me, that I don't know about because I'm a rock of silence.

Director: There's a decent chance. And the more you break silence, the greater that chance will be.

Woman: That's why you talk all the time. You're trying to widen your circle. Why didn't you say this from the start?

Director: I didn't know this was the truth until we said it.

Woman: Now you're flattering me.

Director: No. Some truths only become clear in conversation. Could I have thought this on my own? Yes. But maybe I would have forgotten. I needed you to bring it to mind.

Woman: So it doesn't matter if you thought it before?

Director: What matters is that it comes to mind. Friends are very good at doing this, at bringing things to mind. In fact, that's one of the main reasons to have friends. Does anyone bring anything to mind for you?

Woman: Work related things, sure. But important things? Things touching the soul? No.

Director: Maybe we should be friends.

Woman: We already are.

CLOISTERED

Director: You know the risk, though, don't you? The risk of the philosophical circle.

Woman: Of course I do. You're sheltered from the outside world; you're cloistered. The risk is that you lose touch.

Director: Lose touch with the greater sane.

Woman: The greater sane, yes; and we are the lesser sane. The sane of two against the sane of billions.

Director: Oh, it's not that bad. There might be a dozen of us out there.

Woman: We need to be cloistered to protect ourselves. I don't care about the risk.

Director: And what's the goal? To have the cloister eventually house millions if not billions?

Woman: That's the way the world turns. That's how we evolve.

Director: And if our truth becomes the dominant sanity, we would turn away from it again, cloister ourselves as a handful again?

Woman: Who knows? All I know is that we're few and they are many. Something needs to be done.

Director: So how do we build the cloister?

Woman: We talk. We talk to those who will listen. And we hope we'll connect from the heart, from the soul, from the core of the mind. A circle of friends will grow. I don't care how many. Some is better than none.

Director: Do you think you might find friends at work?

Woman: No. I can just tell even without dipping my toe. There are signs. I promise I'll keep a good lookout, and get into the water if I think I might be wrong. But I see no good in opening up to anyone there.

Director: Where else might you look?

Woman: I was kind of hoping I might tag along with you.

Director: We'll find some friends together. That sounds good. Where will we look?

Woman: I have no idea. Book signings maybe?

Director: Why not? We'll find a good book and go. We'll strike up conversations and see where they lead. Books can be a wonderful basis for friendship.

Woman: It's not so easy to find a good book, a really good book. We should hold out for really good books.

Director: And we will. Maybe you should write one.

Woman: Besides my journals? What would I write?

Director: The life of a first chair violin. Not a biography, but a description of the life.

Woman: And I'd write this in the hopes that I'd find friends? But what kind of friends would I find? I'd have to have some of my soul in the book to find a friend.

Director: Then...

Woman: ...put some soul in. Is that how you find friends? You put your soul in what you write?

Director: Usually I just write for friends. New ones come through luck.

Woman: But if we're going to build a circle, we need more than luck. We need a plan.

Director: I'm not very good at that. Are you?

Woman: I help plan our fundraising events. And there are more than a few. I don't see why my skills wouldn't port.

Director: Find a donor; find a friend. Why not? But there's a problem.

Woman: What problem?

Director: What's our philosophy?

Woman: What do you mean?

Director: Don't we have to have a positive philosophy in order to build a circle of friends?

Woman: What, you mean like idealism, skepticism, hedonism, stoicism?

Director: Sure. Or doesn't that matter?

Woman: It doesn't matter. And I think it's a moot point anyway. Those -isms probably became -isms long after the initial circle formed.

Director: You have a point. But what about in our own time? Ayn Rand founded objectivism and her circle thought of themselves as that -ism.

CIRCLES

Woman: She was a long time writing before that circle formed.

Director: But then what's our circle a circle of other than friends?

Woman: It's a circle of philosophical friends.

Director: Ah. Okay. I can live with that. Some of us will like this -ism; some of us will like that -ism. And our job is to investigate them all.

Woman: Yes. But we won't be primarily taken with -isms. We'll be taken with what we find in our souls.

Director: We'll share, and learn, and make our way. We'll keep ourselves sane. Some things we find we'll deem good; and other things we find we'll deem bad—all with a view toward comfort and health.

Woman: Health, yes. But comfort? Why?

Director: Don't we want the comfort of knowing we're sane? Or isn't sanity a comfortable state?

Woman: Insanity is uncomfortable, sure. Or is it? Aren't some of the greatest lunatics completely comfortable with themselves? In fact, isn't that a sort of definition of insanity—to be *completely* comfortable with yourself?

Director: Maybe that's what philosophers are. And that's what attracts others to their circle, that comfort.

Woman: But there's no way they were always that comfortable. Otherwise, what would spur them to think?

Director: An excellent point. Philosophers find their way to comfort. How's that? Join our circle and find comfort here.

Woman: On the one hand, I completely disagree; on the other hand, I couldn't agree more.

Director: Does that say something about philosophers, or you?

Woman: Both. But I think the point is this. Philosophers start out very uncomfortable with themselves. Then, through very hard work, they grow better. They become happy.

Director: Happy? Are you sure? What is happiness?

Woman: A state of wellbeing. It's what everyone wants. But few are willing to do what it takes.

Director: And our circle will do what it takes. But what does it take?

Woman: We need to clear things up.

Director: How so? Clear so everyone can see inside of us? Or clear as in clear thinking? As Rand would say, after Aristotle—A must be A.

Woman: A is A. I've heard that before. That's a good start, don't you think?

Director: If you can clearly define an A, you're off to a good start.

Woman: How do we clearly define a friend? That's the thing most important to us, after all.

Director: Well, you and I are friends. How do we define what we have?

Woman: We... just have!

Director: We get along.

Woman: Yes, we get along. We share. We can relate.

Director: You can relate to being a philosopher; and I can relate to being first chair.

Woman: No, that's not what I mean. There's something more, something fundamental here. Something... profound we share.

Director: A love for truth?

Woman: Yes, but not quite. You could lie about something and I don't think I'd care. Can you see it that way with me?

Director: You could lie about many things and I wouldn't care.

Woman: But when it comes to the core, that's what matters. Full truth there.

Director: And our circle of friends, philosophic or no, would be honest about the core.

Woman: That's how we'd know they're friends. That's how I know you're a friend.

Director: But now I don't know.

Lies 2

Woman: What don't you know?

Director: I think I'd rather have someone lie to me about the core than lie about the surface of things.

Woman: I don't understand.

Director: The surface of things are the facts we all can know. The core is very hard to see.

Woman: So why make it harder with lies?

Director: If we don't know the surface we trip and we fall. I'd want truth-fulness here. But something false about the core? Who cares?

Woman: I can't believe I'm hearing this from you! Who cares? *I* care!

Director: Why?

Woman: Because I want to know the truth about my friend.

Director: We can arrive at this truth on our own, regardless of what they say. In fact, I think we have to arrive at this truth *despite* what they say.

Woman: Why?

Director: If our friends are in flow, they won't see themselves as they might. And what they do see right, they might lie about in order to flow.

Woman: That wouldn't bother you?

Director: I'd know they were lying from what I can see. But I'd know it was an innocent lie.

Woman: How would you know that?

Director: There's something innocent about true flow. It's something we all want.

Woman: But some of us trample on others to achieve that state.

Director: And they are innocent in that.

Woman: What do you mean? Innocent in trampling others?

Director: The others shouldn't be in the way. Flow is a very personal thing. If you're interfering with someone's flow, you are in the way. Tram-pling is what you deserve.

Woman: I can't tell if you're being serious or not. How do we get out of the way? We pull our feet out of the water?

Director: No, that's not it. We can be fully submerged and not in the way. We simply can't inhibit another.

Woman: Not even if that other is doing wrong?

Director: If they're doing harm, we smack them with a two-by-four. But if they're doing wrong, as in wrong to themselves, we tell them from a distance what they're about—but we don't get in the way.

Woman: Our mistakes are ours to make.

Director: Yes. We have to let them be.

Woman: Why? Why do we have to let them be? Can't we help?

Director: We tell them what they're doing. That's our help. That's all we can do. If they don't listen? Well....

Woman: So we just leave them to their own devices. We let them drown.

Director: If they're drowning, we can lend a hand. But when I was training to be a lifeguard they taught me one thing. If you try to save someone, and they start to pull you under—you punch them in the nose, and swim away.

Woman: There's sense in that. But what does it mean? If someone is lying to you about surface things, things which might pull you under—you lie about something deep?

Director: Well, the metaphor starts to fall apart. But I think the answer is yes.

Woman: Because you value the superficial truth more, and if you lie about the deep, in your eyes, that's not so bad?

Director: Is it so bad?

Woman: It's terrible, Director.

Director: Okay. Maybe I'm wrong. Maybe we always tell the truth about everything.

Woman: Oh, I'm not saying that. I think we have to judge.

JUDGMENT

Director: And what's the basis of our judgment?

Woman: We don't lie about the important things. I think everyone knows this as a truth, regardless of whether they lie or not.

Director: So we always tell the truth about what's important to us. Meaning, if we're trapped by enemies we always tell them our most important truths, assuming they ask.

Woman: Well....

Director: Should we lie to them about our most important truths?

Woman: Would you?

Director: Yes—unless I could get away with the truth.

Woman: Get away from them, sure. But what we're really talking about is speaking truth to friends. You'd always speak truth to me, wouldn't you?

Director: Yes, of course.

Woman: But that's so easy to say! How would I know?

Director: You'd have to judge.

Woman: How would I judge?

Director: You'd have to compare what I say to how I behave. Subtle signs. Overt acts. You'd have to judge it all. And then decide.

Woman: What if I'm so desperate for friends I fool myself into believing you're true?

Director: I wouldn't want a friend who did that. I myself would break things off.

Woman: Even if you were false? Somehow I don't believe you. If you were false you'd seek to keep up the lie.

Director: You're making an assumption. You assume I *want* to be false. What if I *have* to be false? I might value you more for sensing I'm untrue.

Woman: Now that's crazy talk, friend. Who *has* to be untrue?

Director: Someone who harbors dangerous truths.

Woman: If you told me, you'd have to kill me? That sort of thing?

Director: No, not that sort of thing. The danger in the truth is that if it's shared with the unworthy it will be lost.

Woman: Ha! I'm unworthy of your truth?

Director: I think you know what I mean. I'm talking about being ready.

Woman: So what if I'm unready? How does that lose the truth?

Director: There's a force that comes with dangerous unshared truths. If you share them with those who are ready, the force gains in strength. If you share them with the unready, the force is sapped.

Woman: I'm not sure I understand. So what do you do, probe your friends to find who's ready?

Director: Yes. And isn't this really what all of us do? We all probe our friends.

Woman: No. There are some who blabber away and make friends with all and sundry.

Director: Would you guess that *they* have important truths?

Woman: No, I would not. I would judge them incapable of holding such truths. Holding a truth for them would be uncomfortable.

Director: I don't know. I think some of them might hold important truths about themselves. Truths they wouldn't admit—unless someone guessed.

Woman: And you would guess.

Director: Of course I would guess. If I'm wrong, so what? They blabber on.

Woman: But if you're right they shut right up.

Director: Yes. So the question is, do we want them to shut right up?

Woman: Why wouldn't we? That much less noise pollution in the world.

Director: But what happens when a blabber mouth shuts up? One, they grow reflective. Two, they plot revenge.

Woman: Fair enough. You have a point. I think it's rare for them not to plot revenge. And who needs those plotting revenge against them? I surely don't.

Director: Nor do I. But think of this. There might be friends in the orbit of this blabber mouth. We want to break them free. The best way how is to guess the blabber mouth's truth. If we do, we make new friends.

Woman: Who wants a friend given to circling mouths of blabber? I sure don't.

Director: What if they were silent types like you? They circle because they're afraid to open their mouths and speak.

FAIR

Woman: You know that's not fair. I might be silent but I'm not some orbiting moon.

Director: Not even if your conductor were a mouth of blabber? Or isn't that possible? Are all conductors brilliant suns?

Woman: No, they're not. And when they're not it's not fair to the orchestra.

Director: Because all of the orchestra deserves the brilliant sun.

Woman: Point taken. They don't. I do.

Director: How has it gone so far?

Woman: Most of the conductors I've known have been alright. A few of them were great.

Director: Would you want them in your circle of friends?

Woman: It's funny you ask. I don't think I would. I don't want the great in my circle of friends. I want equals there.

Director: The great can't be equal?

Woman: The great stand alone.

Director: So no one in the circle of friends stands alone?

Woman: How would you have it?

Director: We'd all stand together alone.

Woman: While that sounds good...

Director: ...how would it work? What does it mean to stand alone? I think you do it now. The circle of friends asks nothing different of you. It wants you to stand alone. But it wants you to share what that's like.

Woman: What's it like for you?

Director: It would take a very long time to explain. But I'll say this. It's like walking alone in the sunshine or rain, whichever you prefer. You go for your walk, however long it might be—and you reunite with your friends when you're done.

Woman: And that's enough, taking your walk. Who wants to walk alone forever? And maybe you want to take a walk with friends. If you have friends, and they like to walk, walking with them is only fair now, isn't it?

Director: I'm not sure it's about being fair. I think it's a matter of what you want.

Woman: Is it fair to want what we want?

Director: Who cares?

Woman: Do you really mean it? Who cares? Who cares about being fair?

Director: Fair toward whom? Us?

Woman: I meant the others. The *not-us*. Are you indifferent to them?

Director: They're no doubt indifferent to us. What do you think they deserve? Tender consideration?

Woman: No, not that. I don't know.

Director: Could it be that you're not comfortable without a rule of conduct that applies to all?

Woman: Not only *could it be*, it *is*. I am uncomfortable with multiple rules of conduct.

Director: Why? Because that makes you think?

Woman: I think we're on to something important here. Do you have different rules of conduct depending on whom your with?

Director: Of course I do. Most of us do, if that's any consolation. I'm one way toward my friends; I'm another way in audience to the Pope.

Woman: Ha! But I think you're lying here. I bet you'd be the same man with the Pope. But I take your point. If I had dear friends, I'd be different with them.

Director: Is that fair?

Woman: It is. There, are you happy?

Director: I'm happy to count myself as your friend.

COUNTING

Woman: Do you count many as your friends?

Director: There are friends, good friends, and very good friends. I have three to five very good friends.

Woman: Three to five? You don't know something as important as this?

Director: Three I'm sure of, two I have my doubts. So let's count the doubtful as good friends. Three very good, two good, and a bevy of friends.

Woman: A bevy of work friends?

Director: Sure, and others of similar ilk.

Woman: I can't tell if you're being serious or not.

Director: How many very good friends have you got?

Woman: *Very* good? None.

Director: How about good friends?

Woman: Can I count you?

Director: I'm not a very good friend?

Woman: Oh, don't get insulted. Yes, you're a very good friend. Or, at least, I imagine you will be as time goes on.

Director: That's all I can ask. And the rest? The simple friends?

Woman: All the people at work are my friends.

Director: Now, if we're talking about a circle of philosophical friends, how many do we need, and of what sort?

Woman: The circle has circles within. There's an inner core, that maybe has only three to five friends; then there's a middle ring, which has more; finally there's an outer ring of many friends. That's how it seems to me.

Director: Circles within. Are these circles always shifting, or are they fixed?

Woman: The closer inside the more fixed they are. The outer rim is shifting all the time.

Director: Why do you think that is?

Woman: The closer the circle the greater the bond.

Director: Is it that closeness creates a bond, or that a bond draws us close?

Woman: What difference does it make? The fact is that we're close with a bond.

Director: What would break that bond?

Woman: When you have a bond, you count on a person for certain things. If you don't get those things, the bond will surely break.

Director: What kind of things do you have in mind?

Woman: Trust, loyalty, truthfulness, care—those sorts of things.

Director: In other words, what you'd expect of a friend.

Woman: That is what I expect of a friend.

Director: I hope I live up to your needs.

Woman: Needs? You think these things are *needs*? It's how we define being a friend! Do you have a different definition?

Director: I think we should include shared interests. That seems impor-tant here.

Woman: What shared interests do you and I have?

Director: I thought you were taking an interest in philosophy. And I could take an interest in your work. I'm sure you could teach me what to hear.

Woman: But you don't love music the way I love it. Don't protest. I know. As for philosophy, I do take an interest. And maybe that's enough for us to be friends.

Director: I don't claim to love music the way you love it, though I do love certain things. But philosophy has a big enough tent to house both you and me.

Woman: But there's a problem here. You know philosophy better than I. Our friendship wouldn't be on an equal footing.

Director: But you know music better than I. On balance wouldn't we be on level ground?

Woman: Music is a subset of philosophy. I know that much. Yours has greater scope.

Director: You're the first musician I've heard say as much. Isn't there a music to philosophy?

Woman: Maybe there is. What is it? The music of the spheres?

Director: I wasn't thinking that. I was thinking philosophy needs passion.

PASSION

Woman: Why would philosophy need passion? I thought reason conquered all.

Director: Who can reason with no passion to get through the difficult spots? Do lifeless computers reason? I think not. That's not what reason is.

Woman: What is reason?

Director: Passionate truck between heart and mind.

Woman: Are you suggesting there is mental passion?

Director: Mental passion needs to break through to the heart. The heart returns the favor. Open commerce between the two is what we need.

Woman: What comes of that?

Director: Life. Beyond that, who knows?

Woman: That sounds pretty good to me. Music does this, I think. There's a certain math to music, cerebral math. But it speaks to the heart.

Director: But does the heart inform the math?

Woman: It does. It makes us bend the rules—and that's when music is real. Computers make music. It's not real on its own. It takes a heart to drive the machine.

Director: And the machine drives the heart?

Woman: No. The heart can learn from the machine. But it learns how to beat stronger in the end.

Director: Why in the end? Why not now?

Woman: One thing I know about the heart—it takes a long time to learn. Mine does, at least. How about yours?

Director: Mine does, too—if it ever learns.

Woman: Well, that's an interesting question. I'm not sure mine ever really learns. My head learns. I can even tell you what I've learned. But if it goes against the grain of my heart? It's a matter of logic only.

Director: Those who claim logic can overcome all must not have had very strong hearts.

Woman: No kidding. Either that or they try much harder to change the way of their hearts than either you or I.

Director: I don't know. I've spent years and tried very hard, and yet my heart goes back to where it's from. Maybe the best we can do is gain perspective.

Woman: Understanding, yes. And that's important. Understanding is worth the effort. But don't think you can become someone else. Your heart is your heart and will always be what it is.

Director: So we should find ways to accommodate the heart?

Woman: Yes! That's exactly what we should do.

Director: Maybe we can teach the heart better ways to be itself.

Woman: I like the idea. But how do we do that? I think, if anything, we get the mind to stop getting in the heart's way.

Director: So our philosophy is one of heart over mind.

Woman: It is. Mind is the tool. It's only a tool. It serves the heart, our all.

Director: What about the soul?

Woman: Heart and soul are one and the same.

Director: Is heart a simple thing?

Woman: It can be. But hearts can be very subtle, too.

Director: More subtle than the mind?

Woman: The mind merely mirrors the heart. Those without a subtle heart can never—never—have a subtle mind.

Director: Does the heart weigh and judge?

Woman: Better than the mind. The mind can be distracted by so many things. The eye of the heart is on the ball.

Director: But what does this say about philosophy? Or do we just say our philosophy is of the heart and that's all there is to say?

Woman: There's much to say. For one, the greatest philosophers had the greatest hearts. It's of necessity. The heart provides the roots and trunk. Philosophy is merely branches, fruits, and leaves.

FRUITS

Director: I'm surprised you'd leave that much to philosophy. Branches and leaves, sure. But fruits? Are you sure?

Woman: Well, the metaphor is strained. But I'll say this. A fruit is an idea. Good ideas lend comfort and shade to the burning heart.

Director: Now it's a burning heart?

Woman: Of course! What else gets through to the thick headed mind?

Director: Why does a heart burn?

Woman: Because of injustice.

Director: No.

Woman: What? Of course! Haven't you ever had injustice done to you?

Director: I'm not sure.

Woman: How can you not be sure?

Director: Maybe I got what I deserved. Who knows?

Woman: Well, justice is a fruit of the mind delivered to the heart. The mind can bring it about. It's the greatest gift it can give.

Director: Does the heart change under the pressure of injustice?

Woman: Not fundamentally. But things can get complicated.

Director: So it might take an effort by the mind to trace the workings of the heart?

Woman: Oh, yes—very much so. For some it takes a lifetime to figure them out.

Director: But isn't that a waste of time? What if there were a way to cut to the chase?

Woman: I never liked that saying. I don't enjoy those scenes in movies. I like the drama, the interaction of the characters—not some over-done Hollywood chase.

Director: What if there were a way to understand the core of the heart, leaving aside the windings it had to take?

Woman: That would be good and worthwhile, for sure. But how?

Director: The mind must dialogue with the heart, circling ever closer to the core. It must refuse to be distracted by all the many wiles the heart was forced to develop. It can go back and dwell on these things later once the urgent matter is in hand.

Woman: What's the urgent matter? The burning? We want to cool it down?

Director: We want our heart to be warm. If that takes a little cooling, that's what we must do.

Woman: How do you cool a heart? I know the answer. You treat it with the balm of justice. You give the heart what it deserves.

Director: Getting what you deserve is a funny thing. If you're cold, it warms you up; if you're hot, it cools you down. What a wonder this justice is.

Woman: Oh, don't tease. The heart always wants what it deserves.

Director: But who's to say what it deserves? The heart? Isn't that the making of a spoiled brat?

Woman: Then who decides? The mind? The mind is in service to the heart.

Director: Maybe it is—in everything but this.

Woman: So the mind decides what's just and rules the heart?

Director: Don't you think it's good to rule the heart? Or should the heart run wild? Haven't you ever known your heart to want something bad?

Woman: I... have. But I knew it was bad because it would damage the heart!

Director: Who told the heart that?

Woman: You want me to say the mind, but that's not true. The heart knew full well.

Director: So the heart contradicted itself? It wanted what it knew was bad?

Woman: Yes. It wanted to eat the forbidden fruit.

Director: Ah. The tree of knowledge. But does the heart always want to know?

Woman: Are we talking about all hearts, or certain hearts?

Director: We're talking about the hearts that count.

Woman: It's certain hearts, then. And the answer is yes—the heart always wants to know.

KNOWING

Director: When is the heart comfortable? When it's longing to know or when it knows?

Woman: The question doesn't make sense. I don't accept the premise. The heart both knows and longs to know at once. It always does both things. That's what hearts do.

Director: So, for instance, if I want to learn more about the history of the country—

Woman: Is that really what your heart wants?

Director: There was a time when it did.

Woman: To each their own. Okay, so your heart longs to learn of the founding. And then you learn.

Director: And when I learn I might see other areas of history that my heart longs to know. Is that how it goes? One thing leads to another?

Woman: Of course that's how it goes. One thing always leads to another. That's what keeps us going.

Director: But when is the heart comfortable? It always knows; it always longs to know.

Woman: It's comfortable when we act on what we know, and take steps to learn what we want to know. Not everyone does these things, you know.

Director: We have to take care of the heart. We can't ignore what it knows; we can't ignore what it wants to know.

Woman: Exactly. And no, that won't always make us perfectly comfortable. But it will be more so than otherwise.

Director: And that's the thing—being aware of the otherwise. That keeps us on track. Yes?

Woman: Yes, it does.

Director: Is everyone aware of the otherwise?

Woman: I do believe they are. We all have knowledge in our hearts. We've all had times when we don't listen. We've all longed to know. We've....

Director: What's wrong? We haven't all longed to know?

Woman: No, I think we have. But the consequences of not acting on it might not be obvious.

Director: What are the consequences?

Woman: A loss of zest for life. A general malaise. These things don't happen at once. But if you ignore your heart's longing over time, these things will follow.

Director: Can't the head see this happening?

Woman: Like I said, the head is easily distracted. It might not see until it's too late.

Director: Why not act on a longing to know?

Woman: You might have other priorities. For instance, you decide work is more important and never give yourself time to explore.

Director: Where do priorities come from?

Woman: In a healthy person, they come from the heart. In an unhealthy person, they come from others—figures of authority, society in general, what have you.

Director: Follow your heart in all things and be free.

Woman: Yes, that says it nicely.

Director: But hasn't that been a recipe for disaster for many? What about prudence?

Woman: Does the heart know prudence? I think it does. It wants to protect itself. No, the heart will take care of you, if you take care of the heart.

Director: The heart can ask of us some very difficult things.

Woman: And people are afraid, yes. No one is saying life is easy. Following the heart is the hardest thing you can do.

Director: How do you know that? What if there are more difficult things? Like following your head.

Woman: I don't doubt that following your head is hard. It's misguided, is all. Getting your head to support your heart is a very, very difficult thing. But it's all about following the heart.

Director: So you co-opt the head.

Woman: I get it out of the clouds.

Director: Easier said than done.

CLOUDS

Woman: Why do you think people's heads gravitate toward the clouds?

Director: To avoid the tasks set by the heart.

Woman: They're running away.

Director: Of course. Many run. Very few stand their ground.

Woman: So you've come around to my view?

Director: It's not *your* view. And yes, I'm persuaded right now that what you've said about the heart is true.

Woman: I'm glad. But listen to you! Touchy about whose view it is. I had no idea you were so sensitive.

Director: I don't want you to make a mistake.

Woman: What mistake?

Director: To think you can own an idea.

Woman: But people own ideas all the time. They call them copyright and patents.

Director: In philosophy no one owns an idea.

Woman: Not even the one who comes up with it first? I think the whole history of philosophy argues against that view.

Director: Then I'll take issue with the whole history of philosophy.

Woman: Pretty confident in our abilities, aren't we?

Director: I'm just following my heart.

Woman: I hope it's not a jealous heart.

Director: You're very clever. Jealousy does pose a problem, though. Do we follow our jealous heart?

Woman: Hmm. That is a problem. No, we don't. But....

Director: But you're looking for a way for jealousy not to properly belong to the heart?

Woman: Yes. What do you think? Is there a way?

Director: Well, when do we get jealous?

Woman: When someone has something we want.

Director: Like fame for an idea?

Woman: Yes, exactly like that.

Director: We must be mistaken in what we want. We don't really want the fame. We merely think we do.

Woman: Yes, blame it on the head. I like that. But what if you long for it in your heart?

Director: Then the question is whether we follow our heart.

Woman: We... do. Or we get eaten alive.

Director: So what does our heart tell us to do? Destroy the object of our jealousy?

Woman: Well....

Director: So maybe we don't follow our heart. Maybe our head has a job to persuade the heart that it's wrong.

Woman: That will never happen.

Director: So what do we do?

Woman: Count our blessings that our hearts are free of such poison.

Director: It's just too bad for some? There's nothing we can do?

Woman: It really is too bad. We can only hope the jealous get what they deserve.

Director: Before I ask you what they deserve, there must be people jealous of your chair.

Woman: Of course. I've had to contend with jealousy all through my career.

Director: What do those people deserve?

Woman: If it didn't harm others? I'd have them take first chair—and feel the weight of all that responsibility. That might work the cure.

Director: Maybe it's like that for those jealous of ideas. Make them theirs, and see what it brings.

SHOES

Woman: It's all about walking in another's shoes.

Director: But then we're saying the jealous are wrong, that what they think they want isn't what they think. It's something else.

Woman: Maybe we *can* find a way to blame it on the head. The head failed in its role of support. It should have shown the heart what it wanted to see, what it wanted to know.

Director: It wanted to know what first chair violin is like. But it thought it knew. How does that make sense?

Woman: The heart relies on intelligence from the brain. If the brain gives a bad report, it's not the fault of the heart.

Director: Why would the brain give a bad report?

Woman: It's too cowardly or lazy to find out what the heart needs to know.

Director: The brain is the eye of the heart. But I thought we can see with our heart.

Woman: We can. I still think walking a mile in another's shoes is the best cure for jealousy.

Director: There are other cures?

Woman: I spoke loosely. It's the only one. But it's also a highly impractical one. Who can actually walk in another's shoes? What chance is there for that?

Director: Oh, I don't know. Suppose you're jealous of your boss, and then one week your boss is out sick. Their role falls to you. You're very stressed. Things don't go well. There's much more to the job than you had imagined. It cures you of your ill. That's possible, isn't?

Woman: Yes, and that's probably the only way it's possible. I think people overrate their abilities when they don't have to put them in play. What's it called? Armchair quarterbacking?

Director: Yes, it is. It's a common mistake. A very common mistake.

Woman: I also think people underrate the abilities of others who hold lower jobs. These lowly jobs are actually quite hard.

Director: How do you know?

Woman: I worked in a pizza shop when I was a teen. I can tell you—it wasn't easy. You have to juggle twenty things. You're under time pressure all day. You have to stay friendly and polite when you're stressed.

Director: There's more to pizza than meets the eye. But really, Woman. Don't we live in the age of the common man? Doesn't everyone know these jobs are hard?

Woman: Yes, but certain people look down on those who do them—in order to elevate themselves.

Director: I thought you had to be elevated in order to look down.

Woman: You know what I mean. And no, we don't live in the age of the common man. Wealth inequality is as great as it's ever been in the history of the world.

Director: But in a democracy the wealthy are forced to justify themselves to the common man.

Woman: Justification and justice are two different things.

Director: What do the wealthy deserve?

Woman: To give their money away.

Director: How is that a benefit to them?

Woman: Money is a burden to the rich.

Director: Do you really believe it?

Woman: No, but they often do. So give them what they want. Relieve them of their stress.

Director: What's that popular show, where the owner walks disguised in their employees' shoes?

Woman: I know the show. *Undercover Boss.*

Director: If this weren't the age of the common man, how would that show be possible? And what's the moral of the story? The common man has it hard.

Woman: Yes, and then what does the owner do? They give money away to the employees; set up foundations; do other expensive things.

Director: Yes, it makes them feel better—more comfortable with things. Conscience, you know, is a political thing. In an age of aristocracy they might not feel so bad.

CONSCIENCE

Woman: What do you mean conscience is a political thing? And why would you think I know that?

Director: Politics is how we live together. We make arrangements and live by them. If we violate those arrangements, we, if we're healthy, feel a tug of guilt. Conscience.

Woman: It sounds so simple when you put it that way. Maybe it's true. Conscience makes us uncomfortable. So are we saying playing by the rules makes us feel alright?

Director: Part of us, at least. But the rules might be stacked against us. Try as we might things never seem to go our way. That's uncomfortable, too.

Woman: But if we break the rules that keep us down, we feel bad. We're damned if we do, damned if we don't. Is that it?

Director: Pretty much.

Woman: So what's the answer? To learn to feel good in breaking the rules? Is that the philosophy you want to teach?

Director: What if the rules violate the terms of the political order? What if they're not fair? Would you feel bad about breaking them then?

Woman: I wouldn't, no. But I thought the rules *were* the political order. So are we saying that order is unjust?

Director: If you follow the rules what do you deserve?

Woman: Better than most get.

Director: Who says what we deserve?

Woman: I know where you're headed. Everyone thinks they deserve the world.

Director: Not everyone. Some people are aware of their limitations.

Woman: Those *some* are few. So who says what we deserve? Who is objective here?

Director: I'm not sure anyone can be objective here. If everyone is following their heart, what do we expect?

Woman: We need an order that accommodates the heart.

Director: So we can get, in good conscience, what we think we deserve. Does that sound practical to you?

Woman: Honestly? No.

Director: So what can we do?

Woman: We need a practical way of giving everyone what they deserve.

Director: Practical justice. The hardest thing in the world. How do we achieve it?

Woman: Maybe we vote.

Director: Because people can tell what someone deserves. If we enacted that rule, would that sit well on your conscience? Are you comfortable with that?

Woman: Maybe they can tell for lots of things. But the unusual case—you or me—might not fare so well.

Director: Would you recommend a system that does an injustice to you and your friend but gets it right for most everyone else?

Woman: Would you?

Director: No.

Woman: You're adamant.

Director: There's no room for any doubt. A system that's bad for you is bad.

Woman: You don't believe in the greatest good for the greatest number.

Director: I certainly do not.

Woman: You believe in what's good for you and your friends.

Director: Is that a crime? Should my conscience bother me?

Woman: No. But you're taking on the world.

Director: You don't have to whisper. I will always defend my own. Will you?

Woman: I barely defend myself. How can I defend you?

Director: You can speak in praise and blame when the time is right.

Woman: That's all it takes to take on the world?

Director: That, my friend, is much.

PRAISE

Woman: I suppose you have to speak your truth.

Director: That's exactly what you have to do.

Woman: That means you don't just go along.

Director: Going along to get along ends up hurting those you love. Do you need me to explain why that is?

Woman: No, but I'd like to hear you anyway.

Director: When we praise something we don't think is praiseworthy we confuse our friends. The might follow our lead and do the same. This props up something bad and makes it harder for others like us to break free.

Woman: Break free of the bad, yes. And we do this by calling the bad what it is. The bad counts on us to never say what it is. When we say it it's like dynamite.

Director: You clearly understand. The same holds when we praise those who never get praise.

Woman: But they have to deserve the praise.

Director: Yes, and how do we know they deserve it? Integrity.

Woman: What does that mean? I know what integrity is, I think. It's living up to what you are.

Director: I like that definition. What you are—whatever you are. And that's where this is hard. What you are won't be something easily defined. You have to live up to your complexity.

Woman: But also to your simplicity. It's hard to be simple in this world.

Director: So we praise the simple; we praise the complex. We praise whatever is true.

Woman: Do we ever praise the false?

Director: There's a way in which we might, but for our purposes I'll answer no. To praise the false is to feed the lie. The bigger the lie, the harder it is on our friends.

Woman: Is that one way we can know our friends? I mean, if a lie affects me, and I hate it, and I meet someone who feels the same way— that's a good basis for friendship, no?

Director: You're asking if we should stand in praise of common hate. I prefer to praise the friendship. The hate is just a sign.

Woman: Of course. That makes sense. But we should praise those who are open to signs.

Director: Yes, many people violently object to certain signs. These people aren't my friends.

Woman: I don't want to be friends with anyone who violently reacts—to anything. Do you ever react that way?

Director: I sometimes feel the feeling, but I don't let it out. How about you? Do you ever feel violent negative emotion?

Woman: I do. And I don't let it out. But maybe that's not healthy. Maybe we shouldn't praise such terrible self-control. Think of the toll it takes on body and soul.

Director: I don't know. Maybe it strengthens the soul. We have to flex our spiritual muscles to keep things in.

Woman: But the body?

Director: It does create a great deal of stress. It's good if we can blow off some steam by speaking a little, a little in blame of the thing that upsets us.

Woman: We can also praise the opposite of the thing that upsets us. But that seems a little passive aggressive.

Director: Who cares? If someone flatters themselves and this makes us see red, speak in praise of those who are self-effacing.

Woman: Have you ever been self-effacing? Would you like to be praised for it?

Director: My self-effacement is irony, in the classical sense.

Woman: Playing dumb.

Director: Yes. Should I be praised for playing dumb? I don't know. I don't need the praise. Sometimes playing dumb is very amusing, and who deserves praise for amusing themselves?

NECESSITY

Woman: I don't believe it's all that amusing all that often. I think irony is a necessity at times. This is Socratic irony, right? I thought Socrates always set people up. He played dumb them took them down a few pegs.

Director: A lot of people would question the necessity of taking them down. Playing dumb to avoid trouble, sure. Playing dumb to set someone up for a fall? That's... what? Mischievous?

Woman: Maybe. But I still think it might be a necessity if we're talking about making things better for our friends.

Director: You have a very good point. The puffed up and inflated *need* to be taken down. They make things bad for others.

Woman: Yes they do. Now tell me why exactly that is.

Director: They create an atmosphere of untruth. I can't breathe very well in such an atmosphere. I'm very uncomfortable. If we can find ways to clear the air, we should.

Woman: Can anyone really breathe well in such an atmosphere? Even the ones who create it?

Director: I've often wondered this myself. Does taking them down actually make them feel better? Are they relieved? They certainly don't act like they want to come down. But when they do? I really don't know.

Woman: It probably varies from person to person. Some will resent you; others won't.

Director: Yes, I can tell when I'm resented.

Woman: Then you really *do* know.

Director: I don't. Sometimes the resentment fades. I never know if it will. I often don't have the chance to see.

Woman: Are you afraid all of this might catch up with you one day?

Director: Haters will hate. There's nothing I can do.

Woman: I would be afraid. I *am* afraid. I never take people down.

Director: You don't see the necessity. I'm not saying that makes you bad. You just don't see it yet.

Woman: Yet. You think you can get me to see?

Director: I think I can suggest you think about it. Maybe you'll try one day. But I think you'd be gentle.

Woman: Which infuriates them more!

Director: True. When you're calm and cool it really works best.

Woman: Does it? I imagine if I got all impassioned it wouldn't sting as much.

Director: But that's what I meant. Calm and cool stings best. Do you think you can take them down a notch if you don't sting?

Woman: No, I suppose not. I know how to be calm and cool. In fact, that's what most people would say I am. I put a lot of effort into staying calm and cool.

Director: Now do something with it.

Woman: You imply I'm not doing anything now.

Director: You're hiding behind a calm and cool facade. Stop hiding and sting.

Woman: Where should I start?

Director: Who is the most pompous person you know?

Woman: I should really start there? Shouldn't I work my way up?

Director: No, go for gold. Who is this person?

Woman: A member of the board of directors. Not so simple, eh?

Director: I have great faith in you. What's the most pompous thing he does?

Woman: He patronizes me. He calls me his little violin.

Director: That really bothers you.

Woman: It really does. What can I do?

Director: Tell him, in front of others, that you'd prefer if he called you Woman instead.

Woman: Why in front of others?

Director: You want to embarrass him.

Woman: That's dangerous, don't you think? I could approach him privately ask him to call me by my given name. Wouldn't that be more effective?

Director: Would he listen? You want to take him down a notch. You need witnesses for this. They'll think he's bad if he goes on calling you his little violin. He probably doesn't want to be thought bad. So do what you must.

CONTROL

Woman: Are you comfortable when you take people down?

Director: If I weren't, I wouldn't do it.

Woman: Why not? Because you don't like to be uncomfortable?

Director: Because I need to be in control of myself. And I'm most in control when I have a certain level of comfort.

Woman: What happens if you're not in control?

Director: I'll make mistakes. Things will get bad. The best, and worst, kind of taking down is when you only allow yourself so much.

Woman: You mean you can't tell the person they're simply rotten and so on.

Director: Right. Then they write you off. But if you can find a particular thing, and control yourself enough to speak of only that thing, the effect can be great.

Woman: I don't think I have that kind of control. I'm either silent and smiling, or I burn down the village. How do I get your kind of control?

Director: You have to have your own kind of control. And the way you get it is by taking little steps.

Woman: Or making really big mistakes? Be honest. You've made some tremendous mistakes.

Director: How can you tell?

Woman: I don't know. It's just a feeling I get. I think you carry scars.

Director: We all carry scars.

Woman: Not like yours. I just know. But I, too, have scars. They're from mistakes. If I were in better control, I wouldn't have made those mistakes.

Director: You took things too far?

Woman: Way too far. So did you. But we must learn. Learning isn't comfortable, is it? I mean, some people think they're learning while they read historical fiction. And they are, in a sense. But it's not serious learning.

Director: Learning from pleasure is good. We shouldn't be so quick to write it off. But I know what you mean. There is deep learning to be done. And it hurts.

Woman: Superficial learning; deep learning. Yes, the deep stuff hurts. But when you've learned the rewards are great.

Director: What are the rewards? We're comfortable with ourselves?

Woman: We can handle ourselves with aplomb. How I long to do that in truly difficult situations.

Director: Like taking someone down a notch.

Woman: Yes. That's something I really want to do.

Director: You have your member of the board. But I'm sure there must be others in your life.

Woman: Oh, there are. The second chair is always snapping at my heels. He's very full of himself.

Director: Then bring him down.

Woman: But we're not talking about a simple put down. We're talking about having great control so we can influence what they think. Right?

Director: Yes. We want to help change what they think.

Woman: Help? Why only help?

Director: You can lead a horse to water, but can't make him drink. You know that saying, don't you?

Woman: Of course. So we lead them to the truth, and then it's up to them?

Director: That's the best we can do.

Woman: But what about the sting?

Director: Sometimes they need a little shock to help them see the stream.

WATER

Woman: What's the water in the metaphor? Truth?

Director: It could be. I like to think of it as life.

Woman: Drink in life. Why don't people drink in life?

Director: They don't like the taste of water. They need something more. Sugary drinks; alcoholic drinks; fatty drinks like milk.

Woman: The metaphor is expanding rapidly. I don't think I can keep up. But I do like the idea of the water of life. You've given me a drink today.

Director: You've given one to me.

Woman: I have the feeling they'll be done soon.

Director: Yes, it's already past what the doctor told me to expect.

Woman: Do you think that's a bad sign?

Director: Well, I don't want them to rush.

Woman: True. I wish I could pour some water of life into my friend. I'd pour some out for your friend, too.

Director: Thank you. If all goes well, the four of us can get together and have a long cool drink.

Woman: Look! It's the doctor. I have to go to her. I'm so nervous!

Director: Just go.

* * *

Director: What did she say?

Woman: The surgery went well! My friend is in recovery now. I can see her in a few hours. I'm going to go home and shower and put on some fresh clothes. You've got my number.

Director: You have mine.

Woman: Let me know how it goes with your friend.

Director: I will. I hope your friend has a good recovery.

Woman: Yours, too. You know, I really mean it—you gave me cool water to drink while we waited here today.

Director: The pleasure was mine. I'm looking forward to seeing and hearing you play.

Woman: Good. I'll try to give you my best. So I guess it's... goodbye, for now.

Director: Goodbye, for now. And Woman?

Woman: Yes?

Director: Good luck.